Capital Flows and Foreign Direct Investments in Emerging Markets

Centre for the Study of Emerging Markets Series

Series Editor: **Dr Sima Motamen-Samadian**

The Centre for the Study of Emerging Markets (CSEM) Series provides a forum for assessing various aspects of emerging markets. The series includes the latest theoretical and empirical studies from both academics and practitioners in relation to the economies and financial processes of emerging markets. These cover a wide range of subjects, including stock markets and their efficiency in emerging markets, forecasting models and their level of accuracy in emerging markets, dynamic models and their application in emerging markets, sovereign debt and its implications, exchange rate regimes and their merits, risk management in emerging markets, derivative markets and hedging decisions in emerging markets, governance and risk in emerging markets, etc.

The series will be one of the main sources of reference on emerging markets, both within and outside those markets, for academics, national and international agencies, and financial institutions.

Titles include:

Sima Motamen-Samadian (*editor*)
CAPITAL FLOWS AND FOREIGN DIRECT INVESTMENTS IN EMERGING MARKETS

DYNAMIC MODELS AND THEIR APPLICATIONS IN EMERGING MARKETS

RISK MANAGEMENT IN EMERGING MARKETS

GOVERNANCE AND RISK IN EMERGING AND GLOBAL MARKETS

Also by Sima Motamen-Samadian

INTERNATIONAL DEBT AND CENTRAL BANKING IN THE 1980s *(edited with Z. Res)*

EMERGING MARKETS
Past and Present Experiences, and Future Prospects *(edited with C. Garido)*

Centre for the Study of Emerging Markets Series
Series Standing Order ISBN 1–4039–9521–4

You can receive future titles in this series as they are published by placing a standing order. Please contact your bookseller or, in case of difficulty, write to us at the address below with your name and address, the title of the series and the ISBN quoted above.

Customer Services Department, Macmillan Distribution Ltd, Houndmills, Basingstoke, Hampshire RG21 6XS, England

Capital Flows and Foreign Direct Investments in Emerging Markets

Edited by
Sima Motamen-Samadian

palgrave
macmillan

First published in 2005 by
PALGRAVE MACMILLAN
Houndmills, Basingstoke, Hampshire RG21 6XS and
175 Fifth Avenue, New York, NY 10010
Companies and representatives throughout the world.

PALGRAVE MACMILLAN is the global academic imprint of the Palgrave Macmillan division of St Martin's Press, LLC and of Palgrave Macmillan Ltd.Macmillan® is a registered trademark in the United States, United Kingdom and other countries. Palgrave is a registered trademark in the European Union and other countries.

ISBN 13: 978–1–4039–9154–6
ISBN 10: 1–4039–9154–5

This book is printed on paper suitable for recycling and made from fully managed and sustained forest sources.

A catalogue record for this book is available from the British Library.

Library of Congress Cataloging-in-Publication Data
Capital flows and foreign direct investments in emerging markets / edited by Sima Motamen-Samadian.
p. cm.—(Centre for the Study of Emerging Markets series)
Includes bibliographical references and index.
ISBN 1–4039–9154–5 (cloth)
1. Investments, Foreign – Developing countries. 2. Capital movements – Developing countries. I. Motamen-Samadian, Sima. II. Series.
HG5993.C365 2005
332′.0424′091724—dc22 2005043286

10 9 8 7 6 5 4 3 2 1
14 13 12 11 10 09 08 07 06 05

Printed and bound in Great Britain by
Antony Rowe Ltd, Chippenham and Eastbourne

Contents

List of Tables vii

List of Figures xi

Notes on the Contributors xiii

Acknowledgements xv

Preface xvii

1 Introduction 1
Sima Motamen-Samadian

2 The Effects of Capital Flows and Openness on Financial Development in Emerging Markets 5
Siong Hook Law

3 Macroeconomic Effects of Capital Flows: The Case of Mexico 29
Carlos A. Ibarra

4 'Blind Bargaining' and the Effects of Foreign Direct Investment on Recipient States: The Case of Post-Soviet and Eastern European Countries 61
Nataliya Ass and Matthias Beck

5 Foreign Exchange Risk Management in Emerging Markets: The Case of Malaysia 95
Ahmad Shukri Yazid and Mohd Shaladdin Muda

6 Foreign Direct Investment in North Africa: A Comparative Perspective 115
Ahmed Aghrout and Michael Hodd

7 The Impact of Foreign Direct Investment on Trade: Evidence from Tunisia's Trade 133
Rabiâa Mekki

8 Foreign Direct Investment Inflows into Emerging Markets: Driving Forces and Lessons for Africa 145
Honest Prosper Ngowi

9 Economic Growth and Foreign Direct Investment in the MENA Region: A Comparative Analysis 163
Latif Wahid

Index 177

List of Tables

2.1	Definition and sources of the data	15
2.2	Summary statistics and correlations between financial development and various variables	16
2.3	Panel unit root test results for 16 emerging economies	19
2.4	Panel cointegration test results using four alternative proxies for financial development	20
2.5	Alternative panel-data estimation for an autoregressive distributed lag, with interaction term excluded and private capital inflows as proxy of capital inflows	21
2.6	Alternative panel-data estimation for an autoregressive distributed lag, with interaction term included and private capital inflows as proxy of capital inflows	23
2.7	Alternative panel-data estimation for an autoregressive distributed lag, with interaction term excluded and all inflows of capital as proxy of capital inflows	24
2.8	Alternative panel-data estimation for an autoregressive distributed lag, with interaction term included and all inflows of capital as proxy of capital inflows	25
3.1	Cumulative capital flows to Mexico	32
3.2	Descriptive statistics for capital flows to Mexico	33
3.3	FDI in Mexico and domestic demand in the short run, correlation coefficients	38
3.4	Correlation coefficients for current and lagged capital flows to Mexico	39
3.5	Link between capital flows to Mexico and lagged demand and income, correlation coefficients	42
3.6	Further macroeconomic determinants of capital flows to Mexico, correlation coefficients	43

3.7	Mexico: Granger causality tests, I	44
3.8	Correlation coefficients of Mexican investment with current and lagged macroeconomic variables	46
3.9	Correlation coefficients of Mexican consumption with current and lagged macroeconomic variables	47
3.10	Capital flows to Mexico and variation in international reserves	50
3.11	Mexico: Granger causality tests, II	53
4.1	Foreign direct investment inflows into Central and Eastern Europe and Central Asia	66
4.2	Inward FDI performance (PeI) and potential (PoI) indices rankings, 1990–2001	68
4.3	Corruption perception indexes (CPIs) for post-Soviet states	80
4.4	Regression models for a sample of 27 post-Soviet and Eastern European countries, 1998–2002	83
4.5	General least-squares errors regressions for different subgroups of post-Soviet countries, 1998–2002	85
5.1	Companies' reasons for not responding to the foreign exchange risk management questionnaire	98
5.2	Managers' perceptions of major risks for multinationals with foreign exchange risk management	99
5.3	Managers' perceptions of major risks for multinationals without foreign exchange risk management	100
5.4	Managers' perceptions of financial risks for multinationals with foreign exchange risk management	101
5.5	Managers' traits and risk perception – Kruskal–Wallis test	102
5.6	Short-Term transaction exposure managed by ethnic Groups (before the crisis)	104
5.7	Managers' traits and foreign exchange risk management practices – Kruskal–Wallis test	105
5.8	Managers' ethnic groups and foreign exchange risk management strategies	107

5.9	Managers' ethnic groups and foreign exchange risk management strategies – Kruskal–Wallis test	107
5.10	Importance of financial tools in foreign exchange risk management	108
5.11	Currency exposure managed by managers who forecast foreign exchange rates and hedging	110
5.12	Currency exposure managed by managers who did not forecast foreign exchange rate and hedging	111
6.1	Starting a business in North Africa	119
6.2	FDI inflows into Algeria, Morocco and Tunisia	120
6.3	FDI stocks in Algeria, Morocco and Tunisia	122
6.4	Algeria: data	128
6.5	Algeria: growth, government size and skill levels	129
6.6	Morocco: data	129
6.7	Morocco: growth, government size and skill levels	130
6.8	Tunisia: data	130
6.9	Tunisia: growth, government size and skill levels	131
7.1	Estimation of exports equation (7.1) for a panel of six manufacturing industries, Tunisia 1990–2003	140
7.2	Estimation of imports equation (7.2) for a panel of six manufacturing industries, Tunisia 1990–2003	140
7.3	Estimation of individual effect by industries, Tunisia 1990–2003	141
8.1	Policy measures taken by the emerging markets to attract FDIs in 2003	150
8.2	Policy measures to be taken by the emerging markets to attract FDIs in 2004–5	151
8.3	Expected FDI entry modes into the emerging markets, 2004–5	157
8.4	Expected FDI entry modes for Africa, 2004–5	157
8.5	Global ranking of the most attractive countries for FDI inflows	158
9.1	Basic Indicators of GDP, GDP growth rate and exports as a percentage of GDP, by region and country	167
9.2	Per capita income and population growth by region, 1970s–2000	169

9.3 Economic growth rates by region and country, 1980–2002 172
9.4 FDI inflows, by region and country, 1980–2002 172

List of Figures

2.1	Liquid liabilities and interaction between capital inflows and trade openness in emerging markets, 1978–2001	17
2.2	Stock market capitalization and interaction between capital inflows and trade openness in emerging markets, 1978–2001	18
3.1	Non-FDI flows and variation in international reserves	50
6.1	FDI flows: worldwide and developing countries	120
6.2	FDI flows to North Africa and developing countries	121

Notes on the Contributors

Ahmed Aghrout is a Researcher at the European Studies Research Institute at the University of Salford, UK.

Nataliya Ass is a Research Assistant at the Centre for Risk and Governance, Caledonian Business School, Glasgow Caledonian University, UK.

Matthias Beck is Professor of Risk Management, Division of Risk, and Principal Director of the Centre for Risk and Governance, Caledonian Business, Glasgow Caledonian University, UK.

Mike Hodd is Director of Economics and Business Research Cluster and a Professor of Economics at the Westminster Business School, University of Westminster, UK.

Carlos A. Ibarra is Professor of Economics at the Department of Economics, Universidad de las Américas Puebla, Mexico.

Siong Hook Law is a Lecturer in Economics at the Department of Economics, Putra University, Malaysia.

Rabiâa Mekki is a Researcher in Economics at GAINS in the University of Le Mans and a Lecturer at the University of La Rochelle, France.

Sima Motamen-Samadian is Director of the Centre for the Study of Emerging Markets and a Principal Lecturer in Economics at the Westminster Business School, University of Westminster, UK.

Mohd Shaladdin Muda is Professor of Economics at the University College of Science and Technology, Kula Terengganu, Malaysia.

Honest Prosper Ngowi is a Lecturer in Economics at Mzumbe University, Tanzania.

Latif Wahid is a Senior Lecturer in Economics at the Westminster Business School, University of Westminster, UK.

Ahmad Shukri Yazid is Assistant Dean and Professor of Finance at the Sultan Zainal Abidin College, Kuala Terengganu, Malaysia.

Acknowledgements

This volume is a collection of some of the papers presented at the International Conference on Emerging Markets and Global Risk Management in June 2004 in London. The conference was organized by the Centre for the Study of Emerging Markets (CSEM) at the Westminster Business School. My special thanks go to Hanna Scobie, who supported and inspired me in organizing the conference.

I would also like to thank all the contributors for their timely delivery of the chapters and Katie Button at Palgrave Macmillan for her support throughout the period of producing the book.

Last but not least I would like to thank my family and in particular my husband Vahab Samadian for backing me all the way through.

SIMA MOTAMEN-SAMADIAN

Preface

The eight studies presented in this volume are put together to provide a new insight into the role of capital flows and foreign investments in emerging markets. The objective is to identify the array of variables that are influenced by capital flows and the extent to which these need to be focused on in order to maximize the gains of foreign investments. The chapters report on empirical studies carried out on a number of countries in Asia, Eastern Europe, Latin America, Africa and the Middle East and present the latest findings that are important and interesting for all those involved in decision-making in the countries involved and those who are conducting research in the area. In this respect Chapter 2 concentrates on the impact of foreign investments and trade openness on the financial development of 43 countries. Chapter 3 examines the responsiveness of macroeconomic variables to capital flow fluctuations under different exchange rate regimes in Mexico. Chapter 4 discusses the significance of the political stability of states in their bargaining power with multinational enterprises (MNEs), and considers the case of five different groups of post-Soviet states. Chapter 5 shifts the attention to Asia and provides an important insight into the risk-taking behaviour of Malaysian multi-ethnic practitioners. Here the authors, based on an empirical study, report the observance of a specific pattern of risk-taking behaviour that appears to prevail among Malaysian managers in relation to their ethnic background.

The remaining four chapters concentrate on the role of foreign direct investment (FDI) in North African and Middle Eastern Countries and provide interesting reports on the extent by which FDI inflows have affected the economies of various countries in the region. The studies show that African and Middle-Eastern countries appear to lag behind other emerging economies in Asia and Eastern Europe in terms of the size of FDI that they attract. All the studies also highlight the role of political and economic freedom as some of the most important determining factors in attracting FDIs. Accordingly they all argue for the need to adopt various political and economic adjustment policies to improve the chances of the countries involved in receiving FDIs. Overall the volume can be of interest to all researchers and policy-makers who are working on the role of capital flows and FDI in the economic and financial development of emerging economies.

SIMA MOTAMEN-SAMADIAN

1
Introduction

Sima Motamen-Samadian

The role of capital flows and foreign exchange risks in emerging markets has been the subject of numerous studies in recent years. It is widely accepted that foreign investments can have a range of positive impacts on the economy of recipient countries. They are believed to stimulate trade and industry in the recipient countries as well as their financial development and overall employment and income level. To attract foreign investors many emerging economies have embarked on a range of liberalization and privatization programmes. These led initially to large inflows of capital and appeared to help economic growth. The repeated experiences of financial crisis in a number of emerging economies in the 1990s, however, alarmed both investors and host countries about the risks associated with such investments. The sudden outflows of capital in each case exerted acute pressure on the economy of the host country and adversely affected the stability of its foreign exchange market. The economic downturn and the uncertainties that were created in each case drove many investors out of emerging markets. The shortage of capital, on the other hand, compelled the authorities in many an emerging economy to adopt a number of new measures to regain the confidence of the investors, and attract them back.

The present book is a collection of eight studies that demonstrate the role of foreign investments and capital flows in economies of a number of emerging economies in South-East Asia, Latin America, Eastern Europe, North Africa and the Middle East. Each chapter looks at a different aspect of foreign investment and its impact on economy of a different region. In this respect Siong Hook Law in Chapter 2 examines the impact of capital inflows and trade openness, especially in their combined effect, on the financial development of emerging economies. Law employs cross-country and dynamic panel-data techniques on a data set of 43 developing countries during 1980–2000 and shows that financial development is higher when a country opens its borders to both capital flows and trade. The study also identifies institutional quality as another significant determinant of financial development. The findings relate to every indicator of financial development employed (both banking and capital market). They are also robust to alternative measures of financial and trade openness, and to estimation methods and sample periods.

In Chapter 3 Carlos Ibarra looks at the relationship between capital flows and the macroeconomic performance of the Mexican economy before and after the 1995 crisis. Ibarra first tries to explain the evolution of different forms of capital flows to Mexico since 1985, when a series of liberalization and privatization programmes were adopted. He then moves on to examine the effects of indirect foreign investments on consumption and investment demand in the country under different exchange rate regimes. He finds that in the early 1990s, when the economy was characterized by low exchange rate flexibility, both consumption and investment demand were responding positively to variations in foreign investment. The above behaviour, however, changed under the free-floating regime adopted after the 1995 crisis. That is, while the sensitivity of consumption demands to short-term fluctuations in capital flows increased, that of domestic investment demand substantially declined. The above change occurred at the same time when the link between exchange rate and share price index on the one hand and foreign investment on the other hand weakened and lost its earlier strength. The author argues that under the flexible exchange rate regime the real exchange rate and in particular the stock market share price index ceased to be a significant transmission channel for capital flows. Accordingly domestic investment demands became detached from short-term fluctuations in capital flows.

The focus of attention moves to post-Soviet states in Chapter 4, where Natalyia Ass and Matthias Beck examine the role of political stability in the Eastern and Central European countries in attracting foreign direct investments (FDIs). Here the authors point out that FDIs are not necessarily always attracted to countries with a low level of risk and a high level of political stability. On the contrary, they are likely to target unstable countries that are going through a period of transition with high levels of country risk and political instability. In some post-Soviet states the neo-patrimonial nature of rule and the conflict between the genuine economic goals and the private interests of the state ruling elite create high levels of uncertainty and instability for all investors, resulting in a situation of 'blind bargaining' between multinational enterprises (MNEs) and the states. Such cases either discourage the MNEs from getting engaged in a country, or encourage them to seek conditions which are excessively biased in their favour. To assess the impact of political stability on the extent of FDI and the bargaining power of MNEs, the authors make a comparative analysis of five groups of post-Soviet states and suggest that the ability to attract FDI depends on both the indicators of political stability and the level of economic freedom. The authors also show that states that demonstrate greater political stability have a greater bargaining power in their relationship with MNEs and offer them fewer concessions.

Chapter 5 shifts the focus to foreign exchange risk management in Asia. During the 1997 Asian financial crisis, many of the Asian multinationals suffered badly as a result of currency fluctuations. Hence foreign exchange risk management has become an important issue in countries such as Malaysia. In this chapter Ahmad Shukri Yazid and Mohd Shaladdin Muda identify some of the factors that influence managers' foreign exchange risk-taking behaviour. Having carried out a study on the behaviour of 90 corporate treasurers and finance directors of Malaysian multinationals in 3 different time periods – before, during and after the crisis, they found a pattern in risk-taking behaviour of managers that seemed to be related to their ethnic background. That is, while Malay managers tended to be risk-paranoid and attributed greater priority to foreign exchange risk management, Chinese managers appeared to be risk-neutral, and managed fewer foreign exchange risks.

The next four chapters concentrate on North African and Middle-Eastern countries and try to identify the role of foreign investment and in particular FDI in the countries of that region. In Chapter 6 Ahmed Aghrout and Michael Hodd focus on the economies of Algeria, Morocco and Tunisia and the efforts made in restructuring them. They point out how the three countries have embarked on a series of reform programmes since 1980s, though at different paces and intensities, in order to increase the involvement of the private sectors and attract foreign investments. In this respect the authors try to assess the extent by which reform programmes have been successful in attracting FDI inflows into the region. They also examine the evidence for the spillover impact of FDI on economic performance in each country and argue that a minimum level of human resource development is necessary in order to observe a significant level of spillover effects from FDI.

In Chapter 7 Rabiâa Mekki focuses specifically on the economy of Tunisia and tries to establish the relationship between FDI and trade. Using an econometric model, she considers both the FDI and trade by industry, and shows the positive impact of FDI on Tunisia's trade. In particular, she confirms the complementarity between FDI and trade in the case of manufacturing industries.

In Chapter 8 Honest Prosper Ngowi discusses the extent by which the geographical distribution of FDI inflows is skewed in favour of the developed countries, and the degree to which Africa has fallen behind some of the other emerging markets in Asia, Central and Eastern Europe that have recently been attracting larger inflows. He then goes on to explain the main driving forces behind FDI inflows into the emerging markets and underlines some of the lessons Africa should learn in order to attract more FDIs.

Finally Latif Wahid in Chapter 9 examines the economic growth of 11 Middle Eastern and North African (MENA) economies in the past two decades, and shows the extent to which MENA countries appear to have underperformed compared with South-East Asian countries. The author tries to identify the reasons behind the differences in the experiences of the two regions during the last two decades and highlights the role of political and institutional factors that reduced the ability of the countries in the region to attract the abundant pool of international financial resources. In conclusion, he argues the need to adopt urgent political, institutional and structural reforms.

2

The Effects of Capital Flows and Openness on Financial Development in Emerging Markets

Siong Hook Law

Introduction

Financial markets and institutions perform an important function in the economic development process, particularly through their role in allocating finance to various productive activities, including investment in new plant and equipment, working capital for firms and so on. This role has been well researched and documented in the empirical literature, using a variety of econometric techniques. By and large, empirical studies suggest that well-functioning financial institutions and markets promote long-run economic growth (King and Levine 1993a, 1993b; Levine 1997; Demirguc-Kunt and Maksimovic 1998; Rajan and Zingales 1998, Demetriades and Andrianova 2004; Honohan 2004). Levine (2003) provides an excellent overview of a large body of empirical literature that suggests that financial development can robustly explain differences in economic growth across countries. A country with better-developed financial markets tends to grow faster. Thus, establishing well-functioning financial markets and systems, which attract more savings, should be a policy priority for governments. Nevertheless, an interesting question remains: Why, if financial development is so good for growth, have so many countries remained financially underdeveloped? More broadly, why have some economies developed well-functioning financial markets and systems, while others have not?

There are three potential explanations why financial development has been slow in a large number of economies. The first view focuses on the links between law and finance proposed by La Porta *et al.* (1997). Through arduous data collection from 49 countries and careful analysis, these authors have substantially advanced research into the legal determinants of financial development. Specifically, they explore the contribution of a country's legal origin to the formation of its financial structure and its corporate governance institutions. They find that legal origin – be it English common law, or French, German or Scandinavian civil law – partly determines the quality of investor protection and the relative size of the stock market *vis-à-vis* the banking system. They find that English common law systems generally have the strongest investor protection enforcement, followed by Germany, Scandinavian and, lastly, French civil systems. In short, this view predicts that countries that inherited the English common law system obtained a legal tradition that tends to both emphasize private property rights and support financial development.

The second approach to discussing the differences across countries' financial development is represented by the endowment theory of institutions proposed by Acemoglu *et al.* (2001). They argue that the disease environment encountered by colonizers influenced the formation of long-lasting institutions that helped to shape financial development. Specifically, hospitable endowments favoured the construction of settler colonies, where Europeans established secure property rights (for example, Australia, New Zealand and the USA). On the other hand, colonies with high settler mortality rates fostered the construction of extractive colonies, where Europeans established institutions that facilitated state control and resource extraction. Beck *et al.* (2003) examine both the law and endowment historical determinants of financial development, and find that the empirical results provide support for both theories. Nevertheless, initial endowments tend to explain more of the cross-country variation in financial intermediary and stock market development. Recently, the role of institutions in influencing financial development has received attention in the literature. Arestis and Demetriades (1997) suggest that differences between finance-growth causal patterns may reflect institutional differences. Chinn and Ito (2002) point out that financial systems with a higher degree of legal and/or institutional development on average benefit more from financial liberalization than those with a lower one. Demetriades and Andrianova (2004) also argue that the strength of institutions, such as financial regulation and the rule of law, may determine the success or failure of financial reforms.

Though the law and finance and endowment theory are the two leading explanations for the variance in the proficiency of financial depth across countries, a third rationale is, more recently, also gaining momentum. Rajan and Zingales (2003) analyse the importance of interest-group politics in influencing financial development. According to them, politics, driven by special-interest groups representing established business, can explain this uneven evolution of capital markets. Financial underdevelopment may be the outcome of political circumstances – protecting the interests of a narrow political or industrial incumbent. They propose an "interest-group" theory of financial development where incumbents oppose financial development because it produces fewer benefits for them than for potential competitors. The incumbents will shape policies and institutions to their own advantage when they gain power. Incumbents can finance investment opportunities mainly with retained earnings, whereas potential competitors need external capital to start up. Thus, when a country is open to trade and capital flows, it is more likely to deliver benefits to financial development because openness to both trade and finance breeds competition and threatens the rents of incumbents. In other words, open borders help to check the political and economic elites and preserve competitive markets. Globalization forces countries to do what is necessary to make their economies productive, not what is best for incumbent elites.

This chapter provides empirical evidence pertaining to the Rajan and Zingales (2003) hypothesis, namely that openness to both trade and capital flows has a positive influence on financial development in emerging markets. If true, this hypothesis has very important policy implications, namely it calls for simultaneous trade and financial liberalization. This would run contrary to the sequencing literature, which advocates that trade liberalization should precede financial liberalization and that capital account opening should be the last stage in the liberalization process (see for example McKinnon 1991). Besides, understanding the determinants of financial development is important because higher financial development would facilitate economic growth, as shown by the extensive empirical literature.

So far the evidence on the Rajan and Zingales (2003) hypothesis remains limited. The sample of countries used by Rajan and

Zingales themselves, dictated by limited data availability in the pre-World-War-II period, means that their conclusions are, at best, very tentative. Other authors have examined related questions but have not examined the Rajan–Zingales hypothesis directly. Levine (2001), for example, finds that liberalizing restrictions on international portfolio flows tends to enhance stock market liquidity, and allowing greater foreign bank presence tends to enhance the efficiency of the domestic banking system. Chinn and Ito (2002) show that there is a strong relationship between capital controls and financial development. Their finding holds for less-developed countries in terms of stock market value traded, and even more so for emerging market economies. Klein and Olivei (1999) point out that capital account liberalization has a substantial impact on growth via the deepening of a country's financial system in highly industrialized countries, but there is little evidence of financial liberalization promoting financial development outside members of the OECD. In terms of trade openness, Beck (2001) shows that countries with better-developed financial systems have higher shares of manufactured exports in GDP and in total merchandise exports. Svaleryd and Valchos (2002) find that there is a positive interdependence between financial development and liberal trade policies. On the other hand, Do and Levchenko (2004) demonstrate that trade openness is associated with faster financial development in wealthier countries, and with slower financial development in poorer ones.

The chapter is organized as follows. The next section describes the empirical model and econometric methodology. The third section explains the data employed in the analysis and the fourth reports and discusses the econometric results. The fifth and final section summarizes and concludes.

Empirical model and econometric methodology

The empirical model of this study is based on the second and third views of the determinants of financial development from institutions and openness perspectives. Thus, the model specification that employed in the analysis is as follows:

$$FD = f(RGDPC, TO, CIF, INS) \tag{2.1}$$

where *FD* is the financial development indicator, *RGDPC* is real *GDP* per capita, *TO* is trade openness, *CIF* is capital inflows and *INS* is institutions. The *RGDPC* is included as an independent variable to capture the demand for financing. In order to examine directly the hypothesis proposed by Rajan and Zingales (2003), an interaction term between openness and capital inflows is also included in the model as follows:

$$FD = f(RGDPC, TO, CIF, TO \times CIF, INS) \quad (2.2)$$

Equations (2.1) and (2.2) provide the basis for the empirical models that are estimated in this study. All variables in both equations are transformed into logarithm form. If the coefficient of the interaction term is found to be positive and statistically significant, then this implies that the combination of financial and trade openness exerts an influence on financial development, over and above any separate influence that each of these two variables independently may have on financial development.

Panel-data analysis

Rajan and Zingales (2003) point out that their theory can go some way to account for the cross-country differences in, and the time series variation of, financial development. While cross-sectional estimation methods may, in principle, capture the long-run relationship between the variables concerned, they do not take advantage of the time series variation in the data, which could increase the efficiency of estimation. Nevertheless, using time series data may yield unreliable results owing to short time spans of typical data sets. It is, therefore, preferable to estimate equations (2.1) and (2.2) using panel-data techniques, namely panel cointegration and dynamic heterogeneous panel-data analysis. In addition, the data of financial development, trade openness, capital inflows and institutions sufficient for panel-data analysis are available only for 16 emerging economies, spanning the years 1978–2001.

Panel unit root test

Before conducting panel cointegration tests, a panel unit root test is carried out to determine the level of integration of panel-data series based on Im *et al.*'s (1997, 2003) procedure. These authors proposed two panel unit root test statistics, namely the *LM*-bar test and the *t*-bar test based on the individual augmented Dickey–Fuller *t*-values. However, in this study, only *t*-bar test statistics are conducted, since the statistic outperforms the *LM*-bar test (Im *et al.* 1997, 2003). The test statistic is computed as follows:

$$\Gamma_{\bar{t}} = \frac{N^{1/2}\left[\bar{t}_{NT} - E(t_T|\beta_i = 0)\right]}{\left[\text{var}(t_T|\beta_i = 0)\right]^{1/2}} \tag{2.3}$$

where $\bar{t}_{NT}$ is the average of the standard individual ADF unit root *t*-statistics, such that $\bar{t}_{NT} = 1/N\sum_{i=1}^{N} t_{iT}$; $E(t_T|\beta_i = 0)$ and var $(t_T|\beta_i = 0)$ are the common mean and variance of t_{iT} for $i = 1, 2, \ldots, N$, obtained under $\beta_i = 0$, and these two values are tabulated in Im *et al.* (2003: table 3).

Panel cointegration test

For the purpose of testing for cointegration within the panel of 16 emerging economies, the panel cointegration approach proposed by Pedroni (1997, 1999) is employed to examine the presence of cointegration in heterogeneous panels. The main aim of panel cointegration techniques is to pool information on common long-run relationships but, at the same time, allow for short-run dynamics and fixed effects to be heterogeneous across the different members of the panel. Pedroni (1997, 1999) proposes several test statistics based on the residuals of the Engle and Granger (1987) cointegrating regression in a panel-data model that allows for considerable heterogeneity. In this case, the test statistics are constructed using the residuals from the following hypothesized cointegrating regression based on equation (2.1) as follows:

$$\ln FD_{it} = \alpha_i + \beta_{1i,t} \ln RGDPC_{1i,t} + \beta_{2i,t} \ln TO_{2i,t} + \beta_{3i,t} \ln CIF_{3i,t} + \beta_{4i,t} \ln INS_{4i,t} + \varepsilon_{it} \tag{2.4}$$

with tests for the null of no cointegration being based on the residuals $\hat{\varepsilon}_{it}$ using:

$$\hat{\varepsilon}_{it} = \rho_i \hat{\varepsilon}_{i,t-1} + \nu_{it} \tag{2.5}$$

Since the α_i and the various β_i are allowed to vary across the *i* members of the panel, this approach allows for considerable short- and long-run heterogeneity – in effect the dynamic and fixed effects can differ across the individuals in the panel data and the cointegration vector can also differ across members under the alternative hypothesis.

Based on the cointegrating residuals, $\hat{\varepsilon}_{it}$, Pedroni (1997, 1999) developed 7 panel cointegration statistics. 4 of these statistics, called panel cointegration statistics, are within-dimension-based statistics which are constructed by summing both the numerator and the denominator terms over the N-dimension separately. The other 3 statistics, called group mean panel cointegration statistics, are between-dimension-based statistics and are constructed by first dividing the numerator by the denominator prior to summing over the N-dimension. Both panel cointegration tests and group mean panel cointegration tests follow a normal distribution and the asymptotic distributions of these panel cointegration statistics are derived by Pedroni (1997).

Pedroni (1997, 1999) points out that under an appropriate standardization, based on the moments of the vector of Brownian motion functionals, each of these statistics is distributed as an asymptotic standard normal when both the time series and the cross-sectional dimensions of the panel grow large. The standardized distributions for the panel and group statistics are given by:

$$\kappa = \frac{K_{NT} - \mu N^{1/2}}{\nu^{1/2}} \sim N(0, 1) \qquad (2.6)$$

where K_{NT} is the standardized form for each of the seven statistics, μ and v are the expected mean and variance of the underlying individual series used to compute the aggregate test statistics, and these are needed to adjust the seven test statistics to render them standard normal. The values of μ and ν depend on the number of regressors in the model and whether a constant and/or trend terms have been included in the regression model (equation 2.4) are provided in Pedroni (1999). The small size and power properties of all 7 tests for heterogeneous panels are discussed in Pedroni (1997). In general, the size distortions tend to be minor and the power is very high for all statistics when the time-span is long. In terms of power, Pedroni shows that the group-ADF statistic generally performs best, followed by the panel-ADF statistic, while the panel variance and the group statistics do poorly.

Dynamic heterogeneous panel-data analysis

The static panel-data technique based on either pooling or fixed effects, which could be applied to equations (2.1) and (2.2), makes no attempt to accommodate heterogeneous dynamic adjustment around the long-run equilibrium relationship. Careful modelling of short-run dynamics requires a slightly different econometric modelling approach. Therefore, we assume that equation (2.1) (or (2.2)) holds in the long run but that the dependent variable may deviate from its equilibrium path in the short run. In fact, the panel cointegration test is employed to verify the long-run relationship among the variables. To this end, equation (2.1) (or (2.2)) is expressed as the long-run equilibrium relationship as demonstrated by equation (2.4). The ε_{it}'s of equation (2.4) are likely to be subject to serial correlation, but the pattern of serial correlation is not necessarily homogeneous across different countries. The possibility of both serial correlation and heterogeneity raises further econometric issues, which will be dealt with explicitly below.

The parameter estimates of equation (2.4) are obtained by using recently developed methods for the statistical analysis of dynamic panel data, namely the pooled mean group (PMG) estimation. This more recent method is well suited to the analysis of dynamic panels that have both large time and cross-section data fields. In addition, this estimation has the advantage of being able to accommodate both the long-run equilibrium and the possibly heterogeneous dynamic adjustment process.

Embodying the long-run equilibrium relationship equation (2.4) in an otherwise unrestricted autoregressive distributed-lag (ARDL) model for the levels of y and x, and following Pesaran *et al.* (1999), we base our panel analysis on the unrestricted error correction ARDL (p, q) representation:

$$\Delta y_{it} = \phi_i y_{i,t-1} + \beta_i' x_{i,t-1} + \sum_{j=1}^{p-1} \lambda_{ij} \Delta y_{i,t-j} + \sum_{j=0}^{q-1} \gamma_{ij}' \Delta x_{i,t-j} + \mu_i + u_{it}$$
$$i = 1, 2, \ldots, N; \;\; t = 1, 2, \ldots, T \qquad (2.7)$$

where y_{it} is a scalar dependent variable, x_{it} is the $k \times 1$ vector of regressors for group i, μ_i represent the fixed effects, ϕ_i is a scalar coefficient on the lagged dependent variable, β_i' is the $k \times 1$ vector of coefficients on explanatory variables, λ_{ij}'s are scalar coefficients on lagged first-differences of dependent variables, and γ_{ij}'s are $k \times 1$ coefficient vectors on first-difference of explanatory variables and their lagged values. We assume that the disturbances u_{it}'s are independently distributed across i and t, with zero means and variances $\sigma_i^2 > 0$. If it is further assumed that $\phi_i < 0$ for all i and therefore there exists a long-run relationship between y_{it}, and u_{it}, then:

$$y_{it} = \theta_i' x_{it} + \eta_{it} \qquad i = 1, 2, \dots, N; \qquad t = 1, 2, \dots, T \tag{2.8}$$

where $\theta_i' = -\beta_i'/\phi_i$ is the $k \times 1$ vector of the long-run coefficients, and η_{it} are stationary with possibly non-zero means (including fixed effects). Since equation (2.7) can be rewritten as

$$\Delta y_{it} = \phi_i \eta_{i,t-1} + \sum_{j=1}^{p-1} \lambda_{ij} \Delta y_{i,t-j} + \sum_{j=0}^{q-1} \gamma_{ij}' \Delta x_{i,t-j} + \mu_i + u_{it} \tag{2.9}$$

where $\eta_{i,t-1}$ is the error correction term given by equation (2.9), hence ϕ_i is the error correction coefficient measuring the speed of adjustment towards the long-run equilibrium.

Under this general framework, Pesaran *et al.* (1999) proposed the pooled mean group (PMG) estimator. This estimator allows the intercepts, short-run coefficients and error variances to differ freely across groups, but the long-run coefficients are constrained to be the same; that is, $\theta_i = \theta$ for all i. The group-specific short-run coefficients and the common long-run coefficients are computed by the pooled maximum-likelihood estimation. These estimators are denoted by

$$\hat{\phi} = \frac{\sum_{i=1}^{N} \tilde{\phi}_i}{N}, \quad \hat{\beta} = \frac{\sum_{i=1}^{N} \tilde{\beta}_i}{N}, \quad \hat{\lambda}_j = \frac{\sum_{i=1}^{N} \tilde{\lambda}_{ij}}{N}, \quad j = 1, \dots, p-1,$$
$$\hat{\delta}_j = \frac{\sum_{i=1}^{N} \tilde{\delta}_{ij}}{N}, \quad j = 0, \dots, q-1, \quad \hat{\theta}_{PMG} = \tilde{\theta} \tag{2.10}$$

Another panel-data estimation that allows for heterogeneity but imposes no homogeneity is mean group (MG) estimation proposed by Pesaran and Smith (1995). It is calculated based on the mean (across the individual country) estimates of the long run, the short run and adjustment coefficients. This is consistent even under heterogeneity. However, if the parameters are in fact homogeneous, the PMG estimates are more efficient. The hypothesis of homogeneity of the long-run policy parameters cannot be assumed a priori and is tested empirically in all specifications. Thus, the effect of heterogeneity on the means of the coefficients can be determined by a Hausman-type test (Hausman 1978) applied to the difference between the MG and the PMG estimators, where, under the null hypothesis, the difference in the estimated coefficients obtained from the MG and PMG estimators is not significantly different, in which case the PMG estimator is more efficient.

The data

The data set consists of a panel of observations for a group of 16 emerging economies[1] for the period 1978–2001. The countries were: Argentina, Brazil, Chile, Colombia, Egypt, Jamaica, Jordan, Korea, Malaysia, Mexico, Peru, the Philippines, Thailand, Turkey, Uruguay and Venezuela. Four financial development indicators are employed in the analysis, namely liquid liabilities (LIA), private sector credit (PRI) provided by the banking sector, stock market capitalization (MC) and stock market total value traded (VT). All these financial development variables are expressed as ratios to GDP. The main sources of these annual data are the world development indicators (World Bank CD-ROM 2003) and Beck *et al.* (1999).

Annual data on real GDP per capita (RGDPC) are obtained from the world development indicator (WDI) based on 1995 US dollar constant prices. The institutions (INS) data set employed in this study was assembled by the IRIS Center of the University of Maryland from the *International Country Risk Guide* (ICRG) – a monthly publication of Political Risk Services (PRS). Following Knack and Keefer (1995), five PRS indicators are used to measure the overall institutional environment, namely: (1) corruption, (2) rule of law, (3) bureaucratic quality, (4) government repudiation of contracts and (5) risk of expropriation. The above first 3 variables are scaled from 0 to 6, the last 2 from 0 to 10.[2] Higher values imply better institutional quality and vice versa. The institutions indicator is obtained by summing the above 5 indicators.[4]

The trade openness (TO) indicator employed in the analysis is proxied by total trade over GDP, whereas two capital inflow indicators are utilized, namely private capital inflows (PCIF) and inflows of capital (IFC). The definitions of the financial development, trade openness and capital inflow indicators above are presented in Table 2.1.

Table 2.2 reports the summary statistics and correlations between financial development and the various variables employed in the analysis. There is considerable variation in liquid liabilities across countries, ranging from a low of 23 per cent in Argentina to a high of

Table 2.1 Definition and sources of the data

Variable	Definition	Source
Liquid Liabilities/ GDP (%)	Liquid liabilities is the sum of currency and deposits in the central bank (M0), plus transferable deposits and electronic currency (M1), plus time and savings deposits, foreign currency transferable deposits, certificates of deposit, and securities repurchase agreements (M2), plus travellers cheques, foreign currency time deposits, commercial paper, and shares of mutual funds or market funds held by residents.	*World Development Indicators*, 2003
Private sector Credit/ GDP (%)	Financial resources provided to the private sector, such as through loans, purchases of non-equity securities, and trade credits and other accounts receivable that establish a claim for repayment.	*World Development Indicators*, 2003
Stock market capitalization/ GDP (%)	Value of listed shares.	Beck *et al.* (1999)
Stock market total value traded/ GDP (%)	Total shares traded on the stock market exchange.	Beck *et al.* (1999)
Private capital inflows/ GDP (%)	Net private capital flows consist of private debt and non-debt flows. Private debt flows include commercial bank lending, bonds, and other private credits; non-debt private flows are foreign direct investment and portfolio equity investment.	*World Development Indicators*, 2003
Inflows of capital/ GDP(%)	The sum of foreign direct investment and portfolio inflows.	*World Development Indicators*, 2003
Total trade/ GDP (%)	The sum of exports and imports of goods and services.	*World Development Indicators*, 2003

103 per cent in Jordan. Private sector credit, stock market capitalization and stock market value traded also show significant variation. Malaysia has the highest private sector credit, stock market capitalization and stock market value traded, with 94.19 per cent, 114.22

Table 2.2 Summary statistics and correlations between financial development and various variables

A: descriptive statistics

	LIA	PRI	MC	VT	TO	PCIF	CIF	RGDPC	INS
Argentina	22.95	22.68	12.48	2.59	16.92	3.81	1.79	7,189.98	28.38
Brazil	34.35	46.25	14.62	8.73	18.1	2.92	1.7	4,207.72	33.46
Chile	39.64	57.86	50.31	4.68	55.31	7.66	3.55	3595.7	34.91
Colombia	29.2	29.47	7.1	0.75	32.09	3.24	1.76	2,096.08	27.96
Egypt	84.05	35.88	9.37	2.4	53.27	3.37	2.33	946.8	25.57
Jamaica	47.72	29.15	19.22	1.61	100.37	2.19	2.13	1,737.84	26.76
Jordan	102.67	66.65	54.06	7.86	118.87	2.95	1.35	1,692.56	27.11
Korea	58.77	65.94	26.67	47.47	67.29	2.1	1.11	7,964.45	35.47
Malaysia	100.83	94.19	114.22	49.36	146.2	7.06	4.68	3,335.07	37.44
Mexico	27.98	18.82	14.46	6.84	39.51	3.63	2.1	3,291.23	29.44
Peru	24.25	17.14	9.23	2.21	33.21	2.94	2.14	2309.3	23.91
Philippines	43.16	36.98	28.39	8.38	67.61	2.97	1.72	1,101.13	21.49
Thailand	73.79	87.17	27.18	20.1	72.84	3.29	2.29	1,965.95	34.48
Turkey	30.46	18.91	5.11	14.64	34.12	1.93	0.58	2,518.93	29.65
Uruguay	47.77	39.72	0.82	0.05	39.83	2.08	0.83	5,242.98	28.59
Venezuela	39.27	32.91	6.31	1.35	47.92	2.21	1.61	3,593.24	29.14
Mean	50.43	43.73	24.97	11.19	58.97	3.4	1.98	3,299.31	29.61
SD	26.3	24.08	28.3	15.5	36.15	1.66	1	2031.1	4.45
Maximum	102.67	94.19	114.22	49.36	146.2	7.66	4.68	7,964.45	37.44
Minimum	22.95	17.14	0.82	0.05	16.92	1.93	0.58	946.8	21.49

B: correlations

	LIA	PRI	MC	VT	TO	PCIF	CIF	RGDPC	INS
LIA	1.00								
PRI	0.77	1.00							
MC	0.67	0.76	1.00						
VT	0.49	0.70	0.65	1.00					
TO	0.82	0.69	0.82	0.54	1.00				
PCIF	0.24	0.46	0.73	0.27	0.33	1.00			
CIF	0.36	0.49	0.76	0.33	0.50	0.89	1.00		
RGDPC	−0.25	0.06	−0.06	0.34	−0.28	−0.02	−0.18	1.00	
INS	0.27	0.69	0.51	0.68	0.24	0.49	0.42	0.46	1.00

LIA = liquid liabilities/GDP; *PRI* = private sector credit/GDP; *MC* = market capitalization/GDP; *VT* = stock market value traded/GDP; *TO* = trade openness; *PCIF* = private capital inflows/GDP; CIF = inflows of capital/GDP or (FDI + portfolio investment)/GDP; *RGDPC* = real GDP per capita; *INS* = institutional quality.

per cent and 49.36 per cent, respectively. Peru has the lowest private sector credit with 17.14 per cent, whereas Uruguay has the lowest stock market capitalization and traded value, with 0.82 per cent and 0.05 per cent, respectively. Total trade and capital inflows also show considerable cross-country variation. Argentina has a trade openness rate of 16.92 per cent, whereas the Malaysian rate is 146.2 per cent. On the other hand, Turkey has the lowest inflows of capital, whereas Chile has the highest rate with 7.66 per cent.

The correlation results reveal that trade openness and capital inflows are indeed positively correlated with the financial development indicators. For example, the trade openness and private capital inflows have positive correlation with stock market capitalization, with 0.82 and 0.73, respectively. Besides, the financial development indicators are also positively correlated with each other, where the correlation coefficient ranges between 0.49 and 0.77.

Figures 2.1 and 2.2 present the relationship between the financial development indicator and the interaction between capital inflows and trade openness. As shown in these figures, a country more open to trade and inflow of capital such as Malaysia has greater liquid liabilities and stock market capitalization.

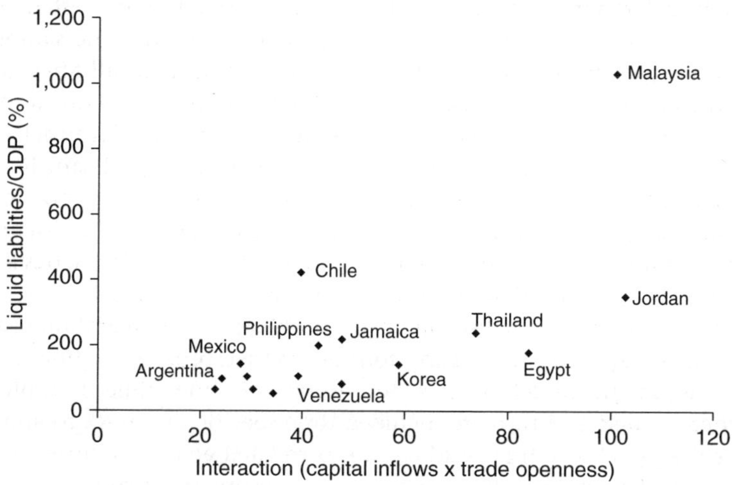

Figure 2.1 Liquid liabilities and interaction between capital inflows and trade openness in emerging markets, 1978–2001

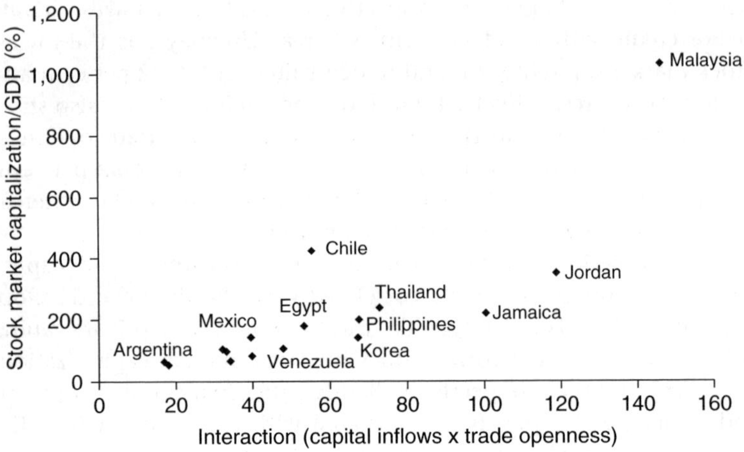

Figure 2.2 Stock market capitalization and interaction between capital inflows and trade openness in emerging markets, 1978–2001

Estimation results

Table 2.3 reports the results of panel unit root test suggested by Im *et al.* (1997, 2003) for 16 emerging economies, with the sample period spans from 1978 to 2001. As shown in this table, all *t*-bar statistics are failed to reject the null hypothesis of non-stationarity at the level for constant with-trend and without-trend models. Nevertheless, the *t*-bar statistics can be rejected at the 5 per cent significant level when estimating first differences. Overall, the panel unit root test results support the presence of a unit root at the level and the absence of any unit root after first differencing. Thus, the panel-data series are stationary at first difference or generated by an I(1) process.

Table 2.4 reports the Pedroni (1997, 1999) panel cointegration tests based on equation (2.5) using four alternative proxies for financial development. Models 1 to 4 are estimates without time dummies, whereas models 5 to 8 are included time-specific dummies to allow for the possibility that residuals are correlated across countries. For four models without time dummies, the estimated results indicate that the panel cointegration statistics reject the null hypothesis of no

Table 2.3 Panel unit root test results for 16 emerging economies (lag length = 1)

	Level		**First difference**	
	Without trend	**With trend**	**Without trend**	**With trend**
LIA	−1.6573	−1.9011	−14.3064*	−13.6322*
PRI	−1.0133	−1.0299	−12.3933*	−11.0436*
MC	0.4432	−1.5585	−7.7226*	−6.1513*
VT	−0.1932	−1.4720	−14.6467*	−13.3519*
TT	−0.6702	−2.0720	−17.4564*	−16.9264*
PCIF	−0.8534	−1.3565	−13.6182*	−13.0295*
IFC	−1.8431	−2.2398	−20.0103*	−18.6522*
RGDPC	1.5237	−2.2829	−18.8944*	−18.6127*
INS	1.6794	−1.9164	−11.6134*	−10.0810*

* Rejection of the null of non-stationarity at the 5% level of significance.
The critical values at 5% significance level are −1.90 and −2.53 ($N = 15$ and $T = 25$) for constant without-trend model and constant with-trend model, respectively. Number of lags was selected using the AIC (Akaike's Information Criteria).

Source: Im *et al.* (1997, 2002).

cointegration. On the other hand, the models with time dummies also reveal similar finding where more panel cointegration statistics reject the null hypothesis. Therefore, the evidence from these panel tests tend to support the presence of a cointegrating relationship among financial development, trade openness, capital inflows, real GDP per capita and institutional quality in the sample of emerging economies.

Having tested for cointegration, the next stage of the investigation is to estimate the impact of openness, capital inflows, real GDP per capita and institutions on financial development using the pooled mean group (PMG) estimations, which imposes common long-run effects. Table 2.5 reports estimates of models (2.1) and (2.2) with four financial development indicators, namely liquid liabilities, private sector credit, market capitalization and stock market value traded. Besides the pooled mean group (PMG) estimation results, the results of mean group (MG) estimators, which impose no restrictions, are also presented. This table presents estimates of the long-run coefficients, the adjustment coefficient, log-likelihood and Hausman

Table 2.4 Panel cointegration test results using four alternative proxies for financial development

Variables: FD, RGDPC, TO, PCIF, INS (lag length 1)

	Without trend dummies				With trend dummies			
Test statistics	**Model 1 (LIA)**	**Model 2 (PRI)**	**Model 3 (MC)**	**Model 4 (VT)**	**Model 5 (LIA)**	**Model 6 (PRI)**	**Model 7 (MC)**	**Model 8 (VT)**
Panel v-stat	2.068*	1.879*	2.234*	0.158	1.932*	1.787*	3.387*	0.544
Panel rho-stat	−1.214	−1.009	−1.807*	−1.465	−1.653*	−1.384	−1.778*	−1.357
Panel pp-stat	−1.929*	−1.669*	−2.177*	−0.335	−2.028*	−2.036*	−2.583*	−0.302
Panel adf-stat	−1.967*	−1.435	−1.640	−0.341	−2.087*	−1.884*	−2.442*	−1.499
Group rho-stat	−1.432	−1.097	−1.469	−1.071	−1.664*	−1.816*	−1.951*	−1.339
Group pp-stat	−1.664*	−1.726*	−1.379	−1.411	−1.392	−1.493	−1.236	−0.341
Group adf-stat	−1.686*	−1.441	−1.839*	−1.444	−1.927*	−1.776*	−1.842*	−1.671*

* the null of no cointegration is rejected at 5% level.
Panel v = a non-parametric variance ratio statistic.
Panel (or group) rho = a non-parametric test statistic analogous to the Phillips and Perron (PP) rho statistic.
PP = a non-parametric statistic analogous to the PP *t*-statistic. ADF = a parametric statistic analogous to the augmented Dickey–Fuller statistic. Rejection of the null of no cointegra tion is one-sided and involves the following:

- Variance ratio: large positive values indicate cointegration (at 5% significance, reject null of no cointegration if $v > 1.645$).
- Other six: large negative values indicate cointegration (at 5% significance, reject null of no cointegration if statistic < -1.645).

test. The comparison between MG and PMG is based on the joint Hausman test. The lag order is first chosen in each country on the unrestricted model by the Schwarz Bayesian criterion (SBC), subject to a maximum lag of 2. Then, using these SBC-determined lag orders, homogeneity is imposed. Owing to the time-span of the panel data being only 24 years (1978–2001), the MG estimator suffers from too few degrees of freedom. The Hausman test statistic fails to reject the null hypothesis and this indicates that the data do not reject the restriction of common long-run coefficients. Hence, the MG estimator

Table 2.5 Alternative panel-data estimation for an autoregressive distributed lag, with interaction term excluded and private capital inflows as proxy of capital inflows

Dependent variable: financial development indicator (trade openness proxy: total trade/GDP and capital inflows proxy: private capital inflows)

	MG estimators	**PMG estimators**	**Hausman test**
Model 1: liquid liabilities (LIA)			
PCIF	0.39 (1.00)	0.22 (1.68)*	1.16 (0.28)
TO	0.65 (0.97)	0.38 (4.28)***	0.69 (0.40)
RGDPC	0.59 (1.59)	0.41 (4.65)***	1.07 (0.30)
INS	1.16 (1.40)	0.34 (3.74)***	1.00 (0.32)
Adjustment	−0.33 (−3.89)***	−0.35 (−3.45)***	–
Log-likelihood	461.15	321.84	–
Joint Hausman test	2.59 (0.63)		
Model 2: private sector credit (PRI)			
PCIF	0.63 (0.14)	0.24 (3.62)***	0.17 (0.68)
TO	0.71 (1.38)	0.33 (2.46)**	2.09 (0.15)
RGDPC	0.34 (0.38)	0.40 (3.83)***	0.00 (0.95)
INS	0.34 (0.26)	0.39 (4.11)***	0.00 (0.97)
Adjustment	−0.53 (−7.00)***	−0.37 (−3.98)***	–
Log-likelihood	365.12	222.99	–
Joint Hausman test	4.78 (0.31)		
Model 3: market capitalization (MC)			
PCIF	0.48 (0.81)	0.52 (2.26)**	0.15 (0.70)
TO	1.46 (0.54)	0.49 (2.34)**	0.52 (0.47)
RGDPC	0.36 (1.08)	0.54 (2.48)**	0.66 (0.42)
INS	1.37 (0.99)	0.29 (2.43)**	1.77 (0.18)
Adjustment	−0.33 (−3.89)***	−0.19 (−4.12)***	–
Log-likelihood	366.02	327.93	–
Joint Hausman test	6.07 (0.19)		
Model 4: total share value traded (VT)			
PCIF	0.44 (0.41)	0.42 (2.83)***	0.04 (0.85)
TO	1.34 (1.86)	0.38 (3.45)***	0.20 (0.65)
RGDPC	0.44 (0.41)	0.24 (4.17)***	0.83 (0.36)
INS	1.15 (1.00)	0.20 (2.12)**	0.01 (0.92)
Adjustment	−0.33 (−3.89)***	−0.49 (−5.33)***	–
Log-likelihood	386.28	341.64	–
Joint Hausman test	0.92 (0.92)		

***, **, *: significance at 1%, 5%, 10% levels, respectively.

All equations include a constant country-specific term. Figures in parentheses are *t*-statistics except for Hausman tests, which are *p*-values.

is not as informative as the PMG estimator for analysis, and we therefore focus on the PMG results.

As shown in Table 2.5, which are estimates without the interaction term between trade openness and capital inflows, the PMG results reveal that the signs of the long-run coefficients of capital inflows, trade openness, real GDP per capita and institutional quality are positive and statistically significant determinants of financial development. The Hausman test for the poolability of the independent variables are failed to reject; this implies that the data of all independent variables can be pooled.

Table 2.6 reports the estimation results of equation (2.2), where the interaction term between trade openness and capital inflows is included in the model. Again, the private capital inflows, trade openness, real GDP per capita and institutional quality are statistically significant to determine four financial development indicators. Interestingly, the interaction term is statistically significant positive at the 1 per cent level and the coefficients are large in all models except in model 1. Overall, these findings provide support to the Rajan and Zingales (2003) hypothesis that openness fosters financial markets development. Simultaneously open trade and capital accounts tend to deliver more benefits to financial development.

Table 2.7 repeats the analysis using, however, the inflows of capital indicator, which consists of foreign direct investment and portfolio investment as a proxy for capital inflows. Again, the joint Hausman test suggests that the PMG results are more appropriate than the MG ones. The results are broadly similar to those reported in Table 2.5. This provides further supportive evidence to the previous finding of a positive relationship between openness and financial development.

Table 2.8 presents the results of the interaction-term model, with inflows of capital as a proxy for capital flows. Again, the trade openness, real GDP per capita and institutional quality remain statistically significant in all specifications, while capital inflow is statistically significant only to determine two capital market development indicators, namely stock market capitalization and stock market total value traded. The interaction term is highly significant in all four models. These findings suggest support for the Rajan and Zingales hypothesis, even when the alternative proxy for capital inflow is utilized.

Table 2.6 Alternative panel-data estimation for an autoregressive distributed lag, with interaction term included and private capital inflows as proxy of capital inflows

Dependent variable: financial development indicator (trade openness proxy: total trade/GDP and capital inflows proxy: private capital inflows)

	MG estimators	PMG estimators	Hausman test
Model 1: liquid liabilities (LIA)			
PCIF	0.01 (0.06)	0.10 (1.18)	0.01 (0.94)
TO	0.40 (5.02)***	0.16 (2.49)**	0.57 (0.45)
PCIF × TO	0.87 (9.96)***	0.23 (3.29)***	0.42 (0.51)
RGDPC	0.21 (1.91)*	0.32 (5.17)***	0.96 (0.33)
INS	0.03 (0.25)	0.12 (2.45)**	0.37 (0.54)
Adjustment	−0.36 (−4.37)***	−0.32 (−4.69)***	–
Log-likelihood	182.46	295.31	–
Joint Hausman test	8.32 (0.14)		
Model 2: private sector credit (PRI)			
PCIF	0.32 (1.37)	0.20 (1.91)*	1.95 (0.16)
TO	0.38 (2.87)***	0.13 (2.48)**	0.47 (0.50)
PCIF × TO	0.38 (0.56)	0.31 (4.15)***	0.06 (0.81)
RGDPC	0.47 (0.64)	0.19 (2.23)**	0.24 (0.63)
INS	0.57 (3.04)***	0.25 (6.60)***	0.38 (0.54)
Adjustment	−0.35 (−3.58)***	−0.22 (−4.18)***	–
Log-likelihood	770.25	673.39	–
Joint Hausman test	7.47 (0.19)		
Model 3: market capitalization (MC)			
PCIF	0.11 (0.49)	0.23 (2.77)***	0.01 (0.93)
TO	0.26 (2.08)**	0.15 (2.41)**	2.44 (0.12)
PCIF × TO	0.24 (1.20)	0.35 (3.74)***	0.01 (0.91)
RGDPC	0.21 (3.07)***	0.25 (5.47)***	0.00 (0.98)
INS	0.36 (2.04)**	0.15 (2.33)**	1.03 (0.31)
Adjustment	−0.37 (−3.26)***	−0.24 (−4.22)***	–
Log-likelihood	804.16	785.95	–
Joint Hausman test	2.68 (0.75)		
Model 4: total share value traded (VT)			
PCIF	0.14 (0.83)	0.12 (2.38)**	1.13 (0.29)
TO	0.28 (3.03)***	0.20 (2.43)**	2.95 (0.09)
PCIF × TO	0.33 (3.98)***	0.42 (6.71)***	0.26 (0.61)
RGDPC	0.05 (0.50)	0.22 (2.47)**	1.46 (0.23)
INS	0.18 (2.57)**	0.14 (2.35)**	5.52 (0.02)
Adjustment	−0.37 (−3.55)***	−0.25 (−4.70)***	–
Log-likelihood	755.25	689.74	–
Joint Hausman test	8.33 (0.14)		

***, **, *: significance at 1%, 5%, 10% levels, respectively.

All equations include a constant country-specific term. Figures in parentheses are *t*-statistics except for Hausman tests, which are *p*-values.

Table 2.7 Alternative panel-data estimation for an autoregressive distributed lag, with interaction term excluded and all inflows of capital as proxy of capital inflows

Dependent variable: financial development indicator (trade openness proxy: total trade/GDP and capital inflows proxy: inflows of capital)

	MG estimators	PMG estimators	Hausman test
Model 1: liquid liabilities (LIA)			
IFC	0.41 (0.95)	0.32 (1.77)*	0.67 (0.41)
TO	0.53 (1.07)	0.27 (2.27)**	1.07 (0.30)
RGDPC	1.03 (0.35)	0.38 (2.90)***	0.38 (0.54)
INS	0.83 (0.90)	0.32 (2.12)**	0.31 (0.57)
Adjustment	−0.33 (−3.89)***	−0.25 (−4.75)***	–
Log-likelihood	380.05	308.80	–
Joint Hausman test	8.42 (0.08)		
Model 2: private sector credit (PRI)			
IFC	0.72 (0.88)	0.27 (2.45)**	0.77 (0.38)
TO	0.92 (1.01)	0.28 (2.41)**	1.18 (0.28)
RGDPC	0.38 (1.05)	0.32 (4.93)***	0.93 (0.33)
INS	1.08 (0.92)	0.31 (2.96)***	0.92 (0.34)
Adjustment	−0.33 (−3.89)***	−0.34 (−3.45)***	–
Log-likelihood	382.72	341.64	–
Joint Hausman test	6.00 (0.19)		
Model 3: market capitalization (MC)			
IFC	0.32 (0.31)	0.33 (3.09)***	1.29 (0.26)
TO	0.92 (0.79)	0.32 (5.79)***	1.22 (0.27)
RGDPC	0.38 (1.37)	0.36 (2.37)**	1.21 (0.27)
INS	1.27 (0.91)	0.13 (2.46)**	0.88 (0.30)
Adjustment	−0.27 (−5.18)***	−0.37 (−4.05)***	–
Log-likelihood	374.36	326.75	–
Joint Hausman test	4.32 (0.36)		
Model 4: total share value traded (VT)			
IFC	0.34 (1.89)*	0.29 (4.58)***	0.05 (0.82)
TO	0.91 (0.87)	0.31 (3.04)***	1.08 (0.30)
RGDPC	0.31 (1.24)	0.25 (3.42)***	0.62 (0.43)
INS	1.09 (0.31)	0.18 (2.36)**	0.70 (0.40)
Adjustment	−0.35 (−5.08)***	−0.44 (−5.57)***	–
Log-likelihood	350.35	318.78	–
Joint Hausman test	1.23 (0.87)		

***, **, *: significance at 1%, 5%, 10% levels, respectively.

All equations include a constant country-specific term. Figures in parentheses are *t*-statistics except for Hausman tests, which are *p*-values.

Table 2.8 Alternative panel-data estimation for an autoregressive distributed lag, with interaction term included and all inflows of capital as proxy of capital inflows

Dependent variable: financial development indicator (trade openness proxy: total trade/GDP and capital inflows proxy: inflows of capital)

	MG estimators	PMG estimators	Hausman test
Model 1: liquid liabilities (LIA)			
IFC	0.56 (0.32)	0.02 (0.23)	0.11 (0.74)
TO	0.36 (1.85)	0.29 (4.79)***	2.45 (0.12)
PCIF × TO	0.83 (1.29)	0.27 (2.54)**	1.42 (0.23)
RGDPC	0.25 (1.23)	0.15 (4.66)***	1.78 (0.18)
INS	0.35 (1.01)	0.13 (2.38)**	1.18 (0.28)
Adjustment	−0.35 (−4.17)***	−0.28 (−4.86)***	–
Log-likelihood	878.33	845.12	–
Joint Hausman test	6.26 (0.28)		
Model 2: private sector Credit (PRI)			
IFC	0.18 (1.48)	0.05 (0.53)	2.36 (0.12)
TO	0.27 (2.16)**	0.25 (5.36)***	1.40 (0.23)
PCIF × TO	0.38 (3.53)***	0.35 (4.14)***	0.12 (0.73)
RGDPC	0.22 (0.92)	0.13 (2.18)**	1.08 (0.30)
INS	0.41 (0.87)	0.11 (3.69)***	0.27 (0.60)
Adjustment	−0.32 (−4.17)***	−0.24 (−3.98)***	–
Log-likelihood	863.21	823.65	–
Joint Hausman test	6.64 (0.25)		
Model 3: market capitalization (MC)			
IFC	0.08 (0.29)	0.13 (3.13)***	0.13 (0.72)
TO	1.34 (6.49)***	0.28 (2.44)**	3.35 (0.07)
PCIF × TO	0.09 (0.61)	0.33 (3.85)***	0.37 (0.54)
RGDPC	0.02 (0.65)	0.22 (2.66)***	0.21 (0.64)
INS	0.33 (1.57)	0.11 (2.29)**	2.64 (0.10)
Adjustment	−0.39 (−4.09)***	−0.26 (−4.19)***	–
Log-likelihood	886.33	857.12	–
Joint Hausman test	5.16 (0.40)		
Model 4: total share value traded (VT)			
IFC	0.46 (0.56)	0.16 (3.02)***	0.24 (0.62)
TO	1.24 (1.68)	0.20 (2.52)**	2.64 (0.10)
PCIF × TO	0.11 (0.53)	0.32 (3.05)***	0.38 (0.54)
RGDPC	1.14 (4.82)***	0.25 (3.56)***	3.67 (0.06)
INS	0.87 (2.04)**	0.14 (2.41)**	4.26 (0.04)
Adjustment	−0.35 (−3.77)***	−0.26 (−4.50)***	–
Log-likelihood	945.69	902.33	–
Joint Hausman test	8.12 (0.15)		

***, **, *: significance at 1%, 5%, 10% levels, respectively.

All equations include a constant country-specific term. Figures in parentheses are *t*-statistics except for Hausman tests, which are *p*-values.

Conclusions

This chapter examines the determinants of financial development from the capital flows and openness perspectives in emerging markets. Although capital flow and openness have been gaining popularity in recent years, there has been no available econometric evidence to trace the link between both variables and financial development. As financial and economic integration become a reality for an increasing number of emerging markets, it is important to understand how the interaction between capital flows and openness affect financial depth.

The panel cointegration and dynamic heterogeneous panel-data techniques are employed in the analysis, where the sample consists of 16 emerging markets and the sample period is from 1978 to 2001. The panel cointegration test results demonstrate that there is a long-run relationship among financial development, trade openness, capital inflows, real income and institutional quality. The pooled mean group results provide support to the Rajan and Zingales (2003) hypothesis – that simultaneous opening of both capital and trade account will promote financial development in emerging markets. The evidence is valid for four financial development indicators and is robust to alternative measures of capital inflows.

The finding also suggests that besides capital flows and trade openness, the real GDP per capita and institutional quality also show statistically significant determinant of financial development. In terms of policy implications, the findings suggest that simultaneously stimulating foreign capital inflows and trade openness, improving institutions and economic development will encourage financial development in emerging markets.

Notes

1. The scale of corruption, bureaucratic quality and rule of law was first converted to 0 to 10 (multiplying them by 5/3) to make them comparable to the other indicators.
2. The correlation results between these institutional quality indicators are high (all are greater than 0.7).

References

Acemoglu, D., S. Johnson and J.A. Robinson (2001) 'The Colonial Origins of Comparative Development: An Empirical Investigation', *American Economic Review*, 91, 1369–1401.

Arestis, P. and P. Demetriades (1997) 'Financial Development and Economic Growth: Assessing the Evidence', *Economic Journal*, 107, 783–799.

Beck, T. (2001) *Financial Development and International Trade. Is There a Link?* World Bank Group Working Paper, no. 2608.

Beck, T., A. Demirguc-Kunt and R. Levine (1999) *A New Database on Financial Development and Structure*, World Bank Group Working Paper. no. 2784.

Beck, T., A. Demirguc-Kunt and R. Levine (2003) 'Law, Endowment and Finance', *Journal of Financial Economics*, 70, 137–181.

Chinn, M. and H. Ito (2002) 'Capital Account Liberalization, Institutions and Financial Development: Cross Country Evidence', NBER Working Paper no. 8967.

Demetriades, P. and S. Andrianova (2004) 'Finance and Growth: What We *Know and* What We Need to Know', in Discussion Papers in Economics *No 03/15*, University of Leicester, UK.

Demirguc-Kunt, A. and V. Maksimovic (1998) 'Law, Finance and Firm Growth', *Journal of Finance*, 53, 2107–37.

Do, Q. and A.A. Levchenko (2004) *Trade and Financial Development*, Graduate Research Paper, Department of Economics, MIT.

Engle, R.F. and W.J. Granger (1987) 'Cointegration and Error-Correction: Representation, Estimation and Testing', *Econometrica*, 35, 251–76.

Hausman, J. (1978) 'Specification Tests in Econometrics', *Econometrica*, 46, 1251–71.

Honohan, P. (2004) 'Financial Development, Growth and Poverty: How close are the Links?' in C. Goodhart (eds), *Financial Development and Economic Growth: Explaining the Links*, 1–37, Palgrave Macmillan, Basingstoke.

Im, K.S., M.H. Pesaran and Y. Shin (1997) 'Testing for Unit Roots in Heterogeneous Panels', mimeo, Department of Applied Economics, Cambridge University.

Im, K.S., M.H. Pesaran and Y. Shin (2003) 'Testing for Unit Roots in Heterogeneous Panels', *Journal of Econometrics*, 115, 53–74.

King, R.G. and R. Levine (1993a) 'Finance and Growth: Schumpeter Might be Right', *Quarterly Journal of Economics*, 108, 717–37.

King, R.G., R. Levine (1993b) 'Finance, Entrepreneurship and Growth', *Journal of Monetary Economics*, 32, 1–30.

Klein, M. and G. Olivei (1999) 'Capital Account Liberalization, Financial Depth and Economic Growth', Federal Reserve Bank of Boston Working Paper no. 99–6.

Knack, S. and P. Keefer (1995) 'Institutions and Economic Performance: Cross-country Tests Using Alternative Institutional Measures', *Economics and Politics*, 7, 207–27.

La Porta, R., F. Lopez-de-Silane, A. Shleifer and R.W. Vishny (1997) 'Legal Determinants of External Finance', *Journal of Finance*, 52, 1131–50

Levine, R. (1997) 'Financial Development and Economic Growth: Views and Agenda', *Journal of Economic Literature*, 35, 688–726.

Levine, R. (2001) 'International Financial Liberalization and Economic Growth', *Review of International Economics*, 9, 688–702.

Levine, R. (2003) 'More on Finance and Growth: More Finance, More Growth?', *Federal Reserve Bank of St. Louis Review*, 85(4), 31–46.
McKinnon, R.I. (1991) *The Order of Economic Liberalization: Financial Control in the Transition to a Market Economy*. Baltimore, MD: Johns Hopkins University Press.
Pedroni, P. (1997) *Panel Cointegration: Asymptotic and Finite Sample Properties of Pooled Time Series Tests, with an Application to the PPP Hypothesis; New Results*, Department of Economics Working Paper, Indiana University.
Pedroni, P. (1999) 'Critical Values for Cointegration Tests in Heterogeneous Panels with Multiple Regressors', *Oxford Bulletin of Economics and Statistics*, 61, 653–70.
Pesaran, M.H. and R.P. Smith (1995) 'Estimating Long-run Relationship from Dynamic Heterogeneous Panels', *Journal of Econometrics*, 68, 79–113.
Pesaran, M.H., Y. Shin and R.P. Smith (1999) 'Pooled Mean Group Estimation of Dynamic Heterogeneous Panels', *Journal of the American Statistical Association*, 94, 621–634.
Rajan, R.G. and L. Zingales (1998) 'Financial Dependence and Growth', *American Economic Review*, 88, 559–86.
Rajan, R.G. and L. Zingales (2003) 'The Great Reversals: The Politics of Financial Development in the Twentieth Century', *Journal of Financial Economics*, 69, 5–50.
Svaleryd, H. and J. Valchos (2002) 'Markets for Risk and Openness to Trade: How are they Related', *Journal of International Economics*, 57, 369–395.
World Development Indicators (2003) World Bank, Washington, DC.

3

Macroeconomic Effects of Capital Flows: The Case of Mexico

Carlos A. Ibarra

Introduction

Mexico has been paradigmatic of the trends that international capital flows to developing countries have followed during the last 25 years. Most of the 1980s were defined by a situation of minimal access to foreign resources and significant 'flight' of domestic capital, as a consequence of the 1982 debt crisis. Later, during the boom of the early 1990s, the country became a major destination for foreign capital. This was a period when portfolio investment in particular, rather than bank loans as had been previously the case, became the major source of non-FDI flows. Finally, the domestic financial crisis of 1995, triggered by the peso devaluation of December 1994, gave way to yet another phase in the evolution of capital flows. While FDI has surged, other types of flows have been comparatively small, though they have shown great volatility, leading to quarterly levels which in absolute terms could be as high as those associated with FDI.

Mexico is an interesting case-study not only because of its rich experience with capital flows, but also because of the country's adoption of different types of exchange rate systems. During the second part of the 1980s, the country basically operated under a predetermined exchange rate regime. This arrangement was given some flexibility with the introduction of a currency band in 1991. However, despite this flexibility, the band system collapsed in December of 1994, and the country woke up in 1995 with a floating exchange rate regime.

Given this background, this chapter has two basic purposes: one, to describe in some detail the evolution of capital flows to Mexico since 1985; two, to analyse the macroeconomic effects of non-FDI flows in particular. In each case, the analysis is organized around a division of periods that feature distinct exchange rate regimes.

Data, periods, methodology

The data used in the analysis are described in an appendix to this chapter. Our basic definition of non-FDI capital flows corresponds to the capital account balance (Banco de Mexico's definition) minus net FDI flows. So defined, capital flows are composed of two main parts. The first consists of bank loans, portfolio investments (in the Mexican stock and money markets) by foreigners, and funds raised in international markets; the second part corresponds to the repatriation of capital by Mexican residents. Naturally, this latter category can contribute to the financial inflows and outflows observed over time; for some purposes, though, it will be of interest to consider only that part of international capital flows that corresponds to funds committed by foreigners.

The period under study is 1985Q1–2004Q2, which, as noted above, encompasses different types of currency arrangements in Mexico. The particular choice of exchange rate regime can be expected to make a difference to the way the economy adjusts to fluctuations in capital flows: for instance, greater inflows may be absorbed through an appreciation of the nominal exchange rate under a flexible system, but through monetary expansion and a fall in local interest rates under a fixed exchange rate regime (see Galindo and Izquierdo 2003 for a recent discussion).

In view of this possibility, we identify two broad periods: 1985Q1 to 1994Q3 – characterized by a semi-fixed exchange rate system – and 1996Q1 to 2004Q2 – featuring a floating regime.[1] The initial part of the semi-fixed-rate period corresponds to a crawling peg system, which later, in November 1991, was replaced by a band regime. A little before this change in regime, in early 1991, a surge in capital flows took shape. For both reasons, in parts of the analysis we consider a sub-period, from the first quarter of 1991 to the third quarter of 1994, and refer to it as the 'band' period.

The facts that (1) we work with quarterly instead of monthly data, because that is the highest frequency available for capital flows, (2) we distinguish between periods with different currency regimes and (3) there is an intermediate crisis period, all together imply that there is a reduced sample size to work with: typically 35 observations for the semi-fixed-rate period (starting in 1986Q1, instead of 1985Q1, to allow for lags in the links between variables) and 34 observations for the floating period. This limited number of observations precludes the use of sophisticated econometric techniques (such as VARs, for instance). Thus, the analysis is based on a series of Granger causality tests, which include the minimum number of lags necessary to yield statistically significant results. These tests are preceded by a discussion of the evidence provided by simple correlation coefficients that already point to some statistically significant links; in this latter case, the inclusion of lags makes it possible to gain some insight into the causal relationships existing between capital flows and domestic demand, and their transmission channels.

The set of potential transmission channels includes: the real exchange rate, the nominal and real interest rates, the CPI-adjusted stock market price index and M2 – as an indicator of overall domestic credit availability. Capital flows, domestic demand and credit are measured as shares of GDP to facilitate an economic interpretation of the coefficients in the Granger regressions. Two definitions of the real exchange rate are used: one corresponds to the consumer price ratio between the USA and Mexico (definition I), the other to the domestic price ratio between tradables and nontradables (definition II). The real interest rate is simply the nominal (Treasury bill) rate less current inflation, both in annual terms.

All variables were Hodrick–Prescott detrended before carrying out the correlation and Granger causality analyses to reduce the possibility of obtaining spurious results. In addition, fixed quarterly effects were removed from the GDP and consumption series, for which these effects were statistically significant. Inflation in Mexico was quite volatile during the period under study, which makes it difficult to arrive at a reliable measure of the real interest rate. That is why the analysis also considers the possible role of the nominal interest rate. This should be acceptable precisely because the series has been detrended: basically, this should get rid of the long-term influence of inflation, and minimize the effect of very short-term fluctuations in inflation that can affect our measure of the real rate.

The rest of the chapter is structured as follows. The second section describes the evolution of capital flows to Mexico. The third and fourth sections analyse the nexus between aggregate demand and capital flows, while the fifth and sixth consider possible transmission channels. Finally, the seventh section presents a summary of results.

The evolution of capital flows

Three distinct phases can be distinguished in the evolution of non-FDI capital flows to Mexico over the last 25 years (see Tables 3.1 and 3.2). The initial phase corresponds to the second half of the 1980s, when there were net cumulative capital *outflows* for US$4.8bn. There were net inflows associated with bank loans (US$10.1bn), but these were more than offset by the outflow of Mexican capital (US$17.6bn). To understand this latter phenomenon, it is helpful to recall that this was a period of strong macroeconomic instability, with an average inflation rate of 90 per cent per year, an annual inflation peak of 177 per cent in early 1988, and large, discrete adjustments in the predetermined dollar parity. Overall, the capital account balance was positive (although very small, at US$10.9bn), despite this phenomenon of domestic capital 'flight', thanks to sustained FDI inflows.

Table 3.1 Cumulative capital flows to Mexico (US$m.)

	1985Q1–1990Q4	1991Q1–1994Q3	1996Q1–2004Q2
(a) Bank loans	10,085	9,238	−37,909
(b) Stock market investments	2,488	26,289	6,839
(c) Money market investments	0	21,419	4,751
(d) International markets	254	25,604	24,826
(e) Mexican assets	−17,632	−3,411	25,672
(f) Non-FDI capital flows I (sum a−e)	−4,805	79,138	24,179
(g) Non-FDI capital flows II (sum a−d)	12,827	82,549	−1,493
(h) FDI	15,708	22,792	118,702
Capital account balance ((f) + (h))	10,903	101,930	142,880

A negative value for 'Mexican assets' corresponds to a net outflow.
Foreign investment in the stock market actually started in 1989Q1.

Source: Banco de Mexico.

Table 3.2 Descriptive statistics for capital flows to Mexico (original figures, US$m.)

	Bank loans	Stock market	Money market	Funds raised abroad	Mexican assets	Non-FDI capital flows	Non-FDI capital flows[a]	FDI
1985Q1–1990Q4								
Mean	420	104	0	11	−735	−200	534	654
Mean absolute value	1,091	104	0	200	1,051	1,156	1,264	654
SD	1,700	202	0	281	1,607	1,621	1,972	250
CV (%)	405	195	n.a.	2,657	219	810	369	38
CC (with non-FDI capital flows)	0.6115	0.5167	n.a.	0.2505	0.6162			
CC (with non-FDI capital flows (a))	0.9848	0.6682	n.a.	0.5816				
1991Q1–1994Q3,								
Mean	616	1,753	1,428	1,707	−227	5,276	5,503	1,519
Mean absolute value	1,773	1,753	1,432	1,707	1,474	5,347	5,692	1,519
SD	2,182	1,532	1,173	1,180	2,173	2,426	3,326	868
CV (%)	354	87	82	69	956	46	60	57
CC (with non-FDI capital flows)	0.3764	0.4489	0.4709	0.3881	−0.0430			
CC (with non-FDI capital flows (a))	0.7291	0.5133	0.2795	0.5261				

Continued

Table 3.2 Continued

	Bank loans	Stock market	Money market	Funds raised abroad	Mexican assets flows	Non-FDI capital flows[a]	Non-FDI capital	FDI
1996Q1–2004Q2								
Mean	−1,115	201	140	730	755	711	−44	3,491
Mean absolute value	1,885	743	489	2,177	2,461	2,372	2,321	3,491
SD	2,468	925	860	2,720	2,833	2,977	2,816	1,881
CV (%)	−221	460	616	373	375	419	6411	54
CC (with non-FDI capital flows)	0.3776	0.1673	0.0333	0.3519	0.5312			
CC (with non-FDI capital flows (a))	0.3312	0.2401	0.1542	0.6041				

[a] Excluding changes in Mexican assets.

SD = standard deviation; CV = coefficient of variation; CC = coefficient of correlation.

Sample for last correlation of 'funds raised ' is 1998Q1–2004Q2.

Sample for first correlation of 'Mexican assets' is 1985Q1–1989Q4.

n.a. = not available

The second phase is defined by the boom of the currency band period. In less than four years, non-FDI flows accumulated a value of little more than US$79.1bn of which the stock market, the money market and funds raised abroad each registered more than US$20bn with a total of US$73.3bn. Notably, the outflow of Mexican capital practically ceased during this period. FDI also increased – reaching a cumulative value of US$22.8bn – but clearly at a much slower pace than financial flows.

Finally, the third phase can be characterized by a dramatic fall in cumulative non-FDI flows: from the first quarter of 1996 to the second quarter of 2004, they totalled less than US$24.2bn; cumulative FDI, on the other hand, rose to US$118.7bn, after the acceleration prompted by the free-trade agreement (NAFTA) signed by Canada, Mexico and the USA in 1994. During this period, portfolio decisions by Mexicans were again a significant influence, although the situation was actually the opposite of that observed during the late 1980s. Foreigners stopped investing in the country in net terms: the (small) investments registered in the stock and money markets, together with funds raised in international markets, were more than offset by loan repayments, leading to a net cumulative outflow of US$1.5bn. Therefore, practically the entire surplus registered in the non-FDI capital account can be accounted for by capital repatriated by Mexicans in the amount of US$25.7bn.

The degree of volatility of capital flows also has changed over time. In the second half of the 1980s non-direct investment flows were quite volatile, with a standard deviation of US$1.6bn, well above their average value of (minus) US$0.2bn per quarter. The situation changed dramatically during the capital surge of the band period. The standard deviation increased to US$2.4bn; however, because there was a steady increase in capital inflows – which registered an average of US$5.3bn per quarter – the coefficient of variation actually fell to only 46 per cent; notably, this is below the 57 per cent figure for FDI, which is usually considered a much more stable component of foreign investment. There was a slight increase in the standard deviation of capital flows after the adoption of the floating regime, which registered a value of US$2.98bn. But in addition, their average quarterly value fell to only US$0.7bn. As a consequence, the coefficient of variation for non-FDI flows surged to 419 per cent. The coefficient of variation for FDI, in contrast, remained basically unchanged.

Thus, in the more recent period non-FDI flows have ceased to be a significant contributor of external resources, but they remain a potential source of macroeconomic instability because of their large volatility. To illustrate: while the mean quarterly inflow of non-FDI capital was only US$0.7bn during the floating period, its mean *absolute* value remained very high, at US$2.3bn. Of course, this reflects the fact that although positive and negative values tend to cancel each other out over time, their absolute value has tended to be high.

What are the components of the capital flows responsible for the observed volatility? Stock and money market investments have not been significant factors during the floating period: not only are their average levels very low compared with those of the other components, but their correlation with the aggregate capital inflow is negligible. Instead, it is the behaviour of loans, funds raised abroad and Mexican assets that accounts for the observed volatility. In particular, the category of Mexican assets shows a high correlation coefficient of 0.53 with total capital flows. If we exclude Mexican capital, then it is the category of funds raised abroad that becomes the more significant factor, with a correlation coefficient of 0.60, followed by loans with a coefficient of only 0.33.

This offers a sharp contrast with the band period, when Mexican assets had a very low contribution to overall volatility; at that time, it was bank loans, funds raised abroad and foreign investments in the stock market that were the leading factors (with correlation coefficients of 0.73, 0.53 and 0.51 with total capital flows, respectively). These changes in the relative importance of the different types of foreign capital, particularly of stock market investments, will be relevant to understanding how the link between domestic demand and capital flows has evolved across periods.

Capital flows and aggregate demand

A basic assumption of this chapter is that non-FDI flows do not affect aggregate demand directly, but rather through their influence on other macroeconomic variables that are significant determinants of consumption or investment (see Gavin *et al.* 1996; Ocampo 2000; Montiel and Reinhart 2001). Given this assumption, the analysis will proceed as follows. First, the evidence on the statistical link between domestic demand and lagged capital flows is reviewed, together with the possibility that this link may have changed after the adoption of the floating regime. Within this broad subject, we also consider the evidence of a possible correlation between capital flows and lagged demand and income, to gain some insight as to the cyclical nature of capital flows.

As a second step, the evidence on the macroeconomic determinants of demand is examined. The set of variables under consideration includes the real exchange rate, the real and nominal interest rates, the stock market price index and M2.

Finally, the statistical link between this set of macroeconomic variables and lagged capital flows is analysed. The idea of course is that if domestic demand is correlated significantly with a variable – say, the real exchange rate – and in addition the real exchange rate responds to lagged capital flows, then that variable is a possible channel for the transmission of capital flows to domestic demand.

The analysis in steps two and three is based on the evidence supplied by simple correlation coefficients between current and lagged values of the relevant variables. This evidence provides the basis for an economically intuitive story; however, the method is rudimentary. The final step of the analysis attempts to circumvent this limitation by performing a series of Granger causality tests according to the procedure explained in the sixth section of this chapter, 'Granger causality tests and transmission channels'.

We start now by looking at the size and statistical significance of the correlation coefficients between the main components domestic demand of and current and up to five lags of capital flows. Although this chapter focuses on non-FDI flows because of their significant short-run effects, for the sake of completeness we discuss very briefly some evidence on the link between FDI and domestic aggregate demand.

Table 3.3 presents the (subset of statistically significant, as in all the following tables) correlation coefficients between the main components of domestic demand and FDI. There are two basic observations to make: first, there is evidence of a weak connection between domestic demand and lagged FDI, with small correlation coefficients (typically not far from 0.30) that are significant mostly at 10 per cent or 15 per cent; and second, the evidence for a significant association is stronger during the semi-fixed-rate period, particularly for investment.

Table 3.3 FDI in Mexico and domestic demand in the short run, correlation coefficients

	Investment (*t*)	**Consumption (*t*)**
1986Q1–1994Q3 (*n* = 35)		
FDI (*t*)	−0.2601+	n.s.
FDI (*t* − 1)	n.s.	−0.2750+
FDI (*t* − 2)	n.s.	−0.3733**
FDI (*t* − 3)	n.s.	n.s.
FDI (*t* − 4)	−0.2868*	−0.2916*
FDI (*t* − 5)	n.s.	n.s.
1996Q1–2004Q2 (*n* = 34)		
FDI (*t*)	n.s.	n.s.
FDI (*t* − 1)	n.s.	n.s.
FDI (*t* − 2)	n.s.	n.s.
FDI (*t* − 3)	n.s.	n.s.
FDI (*t* − 4)	n.s.	−0.3178*
FDI (*t* − 5)	n.s.	−0.2624+

**, *, +: significant at 5%, 10%, 15%.
Investment and consumption are measured as a share of GDP.
All variables have been Hodrick–Prescott detrended.
Quarterly time effects removed from consumption.
n.s. = not significant.

However, in all cases the sign of correlation is *negative*. This is a surprising result even in the context of the recent rise of acquisitions in total FDI (see Mattar *et al.* 2002): if a foreign firm acquires, say, a domestic bank, the operation will generate a positive financial inflow that could be expected to produce a *rise* in domestic demand (see Trigueros 1998). The negative sign of the correlation coefficient, together with its small size and reduced statistical significance, suggest that in fact the observed link is spurious from an economic point of view.

The evidence on the nexus between aggregate demand and non-FDI capital flows is presented in columns 1 and 2 of Table 3.4. As could be expected, the evidence is stronger for the semi-fixed-rate period. Moreover, domestic demand is significantly correlated only with lagged, but not current, capital flows. The effect on consumption appears to be more immediate, taking only one to two quarters to surface; in contrast, for investment it takes 2 to 5 lags.

Table 3.4 Correlation coefficients for current and lagged capital flows to Mexico

	(1) Investment (*t*)	(2) Consumption (*t*)	(3) Real exchange rate I (*t*)[b]	(4) Real exchange rate II (*t*)	(5) Nominal exchange rate (*t*)	(6) Real interest rate (*t*)	(7) Nominal interest rate (*t*)[c]	(8) inflation rate (*t*)	(9) Stock market price index (*t*)[c]	(10) Credit, M2 (*t*)
1986Q1–1994Q3 (*n* = 35)										
Capital flows (*t*)	n.s.	n.s.	n.s.	−0.3262*	n.s.	n.s.	n.s.	0.4651**	n.s.	n.s.
Capital flows (*t* − 1)	n.s.	0.3933**	−0.3952**	−0.3423**	−0.3594**	n.s.	−0.4401**	0.5391**	0.3443+	0.3886**
Capital flows (*t* − 2)	0.3086*	0.2925*	−0.4962***	−0.4756**	−0.5045***	n.s.	n.s.	0.5295***	0.4749**	0.3230*
Capital flows (*t* − 3)	n.s.	n.s.	n.s.	−0.3634**	−0.4001**	n.s.	n.s.	.05496***	0.4548**	n.s.
Capital flows (*t* − 4)	0.2872*	n.s.	−0.3762**	−0.3341**	−0.3881**	n.s.	−0.6032***	0.4685**	0.6448***	n.s.
Capital flows (*t* − 5)	0.4141**[a]	n.s.	−0.3097+	n.s.	−0.3494**	−0.3253*		0.5432***	0.4723**	n.s.
1991Q1–1994Q3 (*n* = 15)										
Capital flows (*t*)	−0.5235**	n.s.	n.s.	n.s.	n.s.	n.s.	n.s.	0.4297+	n.s.	n.s.
Capital flows (*t* − 1)	n.s.	n.s.	n.s.	n.s.	n.s.	n.s.	n.s.	n.s.	n.s.	n.s.
Capital flows (*t* − 2)	0.4331+	0.5444**	−0.4260+	−0.5353**	−0.5139**	n.s.	n.s.	−0.4398+	0.4860*	0.4158+
Capital flows (*t* − 3)	n.s.	n.s.	n.s.	n.s.	n.s.	0.4785*	n.s.	n.s.	n.s.	n.s.
Capital flows (*t* − 4)	n.s.	n.s.	−0.5214**	−0.4333+	−0.4271+	n.s.	n.s.	n.s.	0.5768***	n.s.
Capital flows (*t* − 5)	0.4280+	0.6121**	−0.4470*	−0.5903**	−0.4652*	n.s.	n.s.	n.s.	n.s.	n.s.
1996Q1–2004Q2 (*n* = 34)										
Capital flows (*t*)	0.2762+	n.s.	−0.2774+	−0.2553+	n.s.	0.2819+	n.s.	−0.4338**	n.s.	n.s.
Capital flows (*t* − 1)	n.s.	0.3550**	n.s.	−0.2536+	n.s.	n.s.	n.s.	n.s.	n.s.	n.s.
Capital flows (*t* − 2)	n.s.	n.s.	n.s.	n.s.	n.s.	n.s.	n.s.	n.s.	n.s.	n.s.
Capital flows (*t* − 3)	n.s.	n.s.	n.s.	n.s.	n.s.	n.s.	n.s.	n.s.	n.s.	0.3048*
Capital flows (*t* − 4)	n.s.	n.s.	n.s.	n.s.	n.s.	0.3718**	0.3634**	n.s.	n.s.	n.s.
Capital flows (*t* − 5)	n.s.	0.2991*	n.s.	−0.3392**	n.s.	n.s.		−0.3172*	n.s.	n.s.

***, **, *, +: significant at 1%, 5%, 10%, 15%.

[a] 86Q2–94Q3.

[b] Sample is 88Q1–94Q3 for semi-fixed-exchange-rate period.

[c] Sample is 89Q1–94Q3 (*n* = 23) for semi-fixed-exchange-rate period.

Capital flows corresponds to non-FDI flows, including changes in Mexican assets.

Capital flows, investment, consumption, and M2 are measured as percentages of GDP.

All variables have been Hodrick–Prescott detrended.

Quarterly time effects removed from consumption.

n.s. = not significant.

It is well known that a causal interpretation of these correlations is not warranted. Although the protracted effects observed are consistent with a notion of causality running from capital flows to demand, it is still possible for both variables to be responding to a common third variable (say, a variation in the real exchange rate) that makes them move in the same direction. However, it will be seen that the inclusion of the current values of macroeconomic variables that presumably perform the role of transmission channels for capital flows in the Granger regressions for investment or consumption significantly reduces the measured effect of capital flows on the components of demand. This pattern should not emerge if capital flows and domestic demand were responding mainly to a common shock, and it is consistent instead with the view that capital flows do indeed affect demand through their effect on variables like the real exchange rate (see Iwata and Tanner 2003 for a VAR study of the real effects of capital account shocks in Mexico).

Within the semi-fixed-rate period, the link of consumption with (lagged) capital flows became closer during the band period; the size of the correlation coefficients for investment also increased, although they are statistically significant only at 15 per cent. This closer link is surprising in that it coincides with the introduction of greater flexibility in the exchange rate system. But it should be considered that at the time there was a surge in capital inflows, which is known to have induced a consumption boom (Lustig and Ros 1999). The finding is also understandable if we recall that, although formally there was a relatively wide exchange rate band, in practice there was a much narrower intervention band that the central bank relied on to guide its daily operations in the market, and which severely reduced the actual variability of the exchange rate (Schwartz 1994; see Svensson 1992 for a general discussion on the issue of intra-marginal intervention).

The link between capital flows and domestic demand became much weaker during the floating period, particularly for investment (with a fall in the correlation coefficient from 0.40 to 0.28). Moreover, the correlation is contemporaneous, which also suggests that the link is weak, or maybe spurious: one would expect the effect of capital flows on investment to take some time to materialize. This initial finding will be confirmed later by the estimation of Granger causality regressions. The link with consumption also tended to become weaker after the introduction of the floating system; however, if we consider the entire semi-fixed-rate period, there is basically no change in the correlation coefficients. This is remarkable in view of the very different exchange rate regimes in operation. Thus, while a disconnection of domestic investment from capital flows has taken place in the recent period, no such pattern can be clearly detected for consumption.

The cyclical character of capital flows

The estimated correlation coefficients suggest that there is a causal relationship going from capital flows to demand. It is also possible, however, to look for a possible link between capital flows and lagged demand or lagged income, which would be important for assessing the likely cyclical role of capital flows. Say an increase in domestic demand takes place; if next there is an increase in capital inflows, this will reinforce the demand boom in pro-cyclical fashion. Alternatively, consider a fall in domestic income that tends to depress local demand. If capital flows react negatively to income, in this case they will rise and play an anti-cyclical role, in particular by facilitating a disconnection of domestic demand from short-run variations in domestic income.

Table 3.5 (columns 1 and 2) shows the estimated correlation coefficients of capital flows with lagged output levels and annual (Q/Q) growth rates. The correlation coefficients are significantly positive in both the semi-fixed and floating-rate periods, signalling a pro-cyclical character of capital flows (see Prasad *et al.* 2003 for international evidence). The table shows that the same pro-cyclical response takes place for investment or consumption, although for the latter the response is significant only during the semi-fixed-rate period.

Presumably, capital flows react to variations in other macroeconomic variables besides output and demand. Table 3.6 (column 3) shows, for example, that there is a negative correlation between capital flows and lagged levels of the nominal interest rate. Why? One possible explanation recalls the debates that followed the South-East Asian crisis of the late 1990s, when it was argued that a monetary tightening may be counterproductive and produce further currency depreciation. The reasoning was that the tightening could destabilize the domestic macroeconomy and create a problem of lack of credibility among international investors (Furman and Stiglitz 1998), where upon we would find the observed result of a rise in the interest rate followed by a fall in capital inflows.

Table 3.5 Link between capital flows to Mexico and lagged demand and income, correlation coefficients

	(1) Output (*t*)	(2) Output growth (*t*)	(3) Investment (*t*)	(4) Consumption (*t*)
1986Q1–1994Q3				
Capital flows (*t*)	0.2588+	n.s.	n.s.	n.s.
Capital flows (*t* + 1)	0.3061*	n.s.	n.s.	n.s.
Capital flows (*t* + 2)	n.s.	n.s.	0.3168*	n.s.
Capital flows (*t* + 3)	0.3526**	n.s.	0.3881**	0.4950***[a]
Capital flows (*t* + 4)	0.5774***	0.4682***	0.4653***	n.s.
1996Q1–2004Q2				
Capital flows (*t*)	n.s.	n.s.	0.2762+	n.s.
Capital flows (*t* + 1)	0.3433**	n.s.	0.5213***	n.s.
Capital flows (*t* + 2)	0.2780+	n.s.	0.2925*	n.s.
Capital flows (*t* + 3)	0.2563+	0.3108*	n.s.	n.s.
Capital flows (*t* + 4)	n.s.	n.s.	0.2920*	n.s.

[a] Sample 87Q1–94Q3.
***, **, *, +: significant at 1%, 5%, 10%, 15%.
Capital flows correspond to non-FDI flows, including changes in Mexican assets.
Output corresponds to the natural log of GDP.
Output growth is the Q/Q percentage rate of change of GDP.
Capital flows, investment and consumption are measured as percentage shares of GDP.
Quarterly time effects have been removed from consumption.
All variables except output growth have been Hodrick–Prescott detrended.

An alternative explanation, however, is simply that the nominal interest rate is capturing changes in the overall macroeconomic environment: a fall in the interest rate would reflect a better environment (recall that Mexico has been in a disinflation process throughout most of the period under analysis) to which investors would react favourably. This second interpretation is in fact supported by the observation that correlation with the *real* interest rate is positive; that is, the reaction of capital flows to a rise in interest rates, after controlling for inflation, is positive.

Another finding is that capital flows react negatively to the real exchange rate (see Table 3.6, columns 1 and 2), opening the door to bandwagon-type effects: a real currency appreciation (a fall in the real exchange rate) leads to improved expectations and a rise in capital inflows, which in turn lead to further currency appreciation (return to Table 3.4, columns 3 and 4). Because both capital flows and domestic demand may respond to variables like the exchange and

Table 3.6 Further macroeconomic determinants of capital flows to Mexico, correlation coefficients

	(1) Real exchange rate I (t)	(2) Real exchange rate II (t)	(3) Nominal interest rate (t)	(4) Real interest rate (t)
1986Q1–1994Q3				
Capital flows (t)	n.s.	−0.3262*	n.s.	n.s.
Capital flows (t + 1)	n.s.	−0.2969*	n.s.	n.s.
Capital flows (t + 2)	n.s.	−0.3798**	n.s.	0.4114**
Capital flows (t + 3)	−0.3298*	−0.3505**	−0.2821+	0.2956+
Capital flows (t + 4)	−0.4050**	−0.2493+	−0.4879***	n.s.
1996Q1–2004Q2				
Capital flows (t)	−0.2774+	−0.2553+	n.s.	0.2819+
Capital flows (t + 1)	−0.3880**	n.s.	−0.3825**	n.s.
Capital flows (t + 2)	−0.4417***	−0.3133*	−0.4162**	n.s.
Capital flows (t + 3)	−0.3267**	−0.2762+	−0.3926**	n.s.
Capital flows (t + 4)	−0.3711**	n.s.	−0.3176*	n.s.

***, **, *, +: significant at 1%, 5%, 10%, 15%.
Capital flows correspond to non-FDI flows, including changes in Mexican assets.
Capital flows are measured as a percentage share of GDP.
Quarterly time effects have been removed from consumption.
All variables have been Hodrick–Prescott detrended.
n.s. = not significant.

the interest rates, there is the possibility that the observed correlation of capital flows with lagged demand may be spurious. For example, an appreciation of the real exchange rate may lead to both greater investment (consumption, aggregate income) and capital inflows. To examine this possibility, Table 3.7 reports the results of Granger causality tests for the hypothesis that all coefficients of lagged income (or investment or consumption) are equal to zero. The dependent variable is capital flows, while the right-hand side includes the lagged values of capital flows income or demand of the real exchange rate and the real interest rate. Contrasting the results from this benchmark specification with those of equations excluding the real interest rate did not show much change; in contrast, the role of the exchange rate was particularly suggestive.

Simple correlation coefficients between capital flows and lagged GDP had suggested that output caused capital flows, with relatively weaker support for the floating period. Estimation of the Granger equations provides clues to the nature of this link. During the semi-fixed

Table 3.7 Mexico: Granger causality tests, I

	Number of lags			
Null hypothesis	**1**	**2**	**3**	**4**
1987Q1–1994Q3				
(1) Output does not Granger cause capital flows	0.2150	0.6203	0.9347	0.0549+
(2) (equation excluding real exchange rate)	0.1222+	0.1390+	0.4066	0.0002+
(3) Investment does not Granger cause capital flows	0.7909	0.0761+	0.6543	0.0446+
(4) (equation excluding real exchange rate)	0.4547	0.0083+	0.0597+	0.0420+
(5) Consumption does not Granger cause capital flows	0.5853	0.4005	0.2102	0.4673
1996Q1–2004Q2				
(6) Output does not Granger cause capital flows	0.5265	0.9214	0.5689	0.3531
(7) (equation excluding real exchange rate)	0.0529+	0.1319+	0.4023	0.6033
(8) Investment does not Granger cause capital flows	0.0112+	0.2843	0.2056	0.0321
(9) (equation excluding real exchange rate)	0.0002+	0.0010+	0.0048+	0.0201+
(10) Consumption does not Granger cause capital flows	0.3241	0.0842–	0.1503–	0.1072–
(11) (equation excluding real exchange rate)	0.7699	0.7197	0.5311	0.5802

Capital flows correspond to non-FDI flows, including changes in Mexican assets.
Equations include lagged values of the real exchange rate I and the real interest rate, in addition to capital flows and output (or investment or consumption).
Reported *p*-values correspond to the null hypothesis that all coefficients on output, investment or consumption are zero.
A plus sign (+) means the sum of coefficients is positive; a minus sign (–) indicates that it is negative.

period, non-causality from output to capital flows can be rejected at approximately 5 per cent of significance in a regression with 4 lags (see Table 3.7, row 1). Thus, capital flows reacted to output variations even after controlling for the exchange rate and the interest rate.

In contrast, non-causality from output cannot be rejected during the floating period, irrespective of the number of lags included in the equation; however, non-causality is rejected at nearly 5 per cent of significance when the real exchange rate is removed (row 7). This is consistent with the idea that in fact no direct response of capital flows to past income has taken place during the floating period, but rather that the positive link observed is being caused by the common influence of the real exchange rate on both variables.

With respect to investment, the estimated correlation coefficients suggested that capital flows reacted positively during both periods, with slightly larger correlation coefficients and shorter lags in the response during the floating period. Granger causality tests show that, although the real exchange rate may have been a common third variable behind capital flows and investment during the semi-fixed period (see in particular the equation with 3 lags in Table 3.7, rows 3 and 4), investment *per se* was a cause of capital flows (see the equations with 2 and 4 lags that include the real exchange rate and the real interest rate). A similar reasoning applies to the floating period.

The case of consumption yields further insights. It will be recalled that simple correlation coefficients failed to detect a significant link between lagged consumption and capital flows during the floating period. Table 3.7 (row 11) shows that when the real exchange rate is excluded, there is indeed strong support for the non-causality hypothesis; however, the non-causality hypothesis can be rejected, at approximately 10 per cent of significance, when the real exchange rate *is* included. Moreover, the sign of the sum of coefficients is negative. This means that capital flows have been counter-cyclical in relation to consumption. The absence of a significant link between past consumption and capital flows in the former specification could be explained as follows. Suppose that a fall in consumption does lead to a larger capital inflow. But consider that a rise in the real exchange rate tends to produce a fall in both consumption and capital flows. This latter fall would tend to offset the rise in capital flows directly produced by the decline in consumption, leading to the (false) observation of a lack of significant nexus between capital flows and lagged consumption.

Aspects of macroeconomic adjustment

If domestic demand is significantly correlated with lagged capital flows, what are the likely transmission channels? To approach this issue, Tables 3.8 and 3.9 start by presenting the estimated correlation coefficients of investment and consumption with a set of potential macroeconomic determinants, which include, as mentioned: the real

Table 3.8 Correlation coefficients of Mexican investment with current and lagged macroeconomic variables

	(1) Real exchange rate I	(2) Real exchange rate II	(3) Real interest rate	(4) Nominal interest rate	(5) Stock market price index	(6) Credit, M2
1986Q1–1994Q3						
t	−0.6549***	−0.5205***	−0.6629***	−0.4428***	0.3601**	n.s.
$t-1$	−0.6316***	−0.4432***	−0.6051***	−0.4074**	0.4033**	n.s.
$t-2$	−0.5379***	−0.3594**	n.s.	n.s.	0.3366**	n.s.
$t-3$	−0.3787**	n.s.	n.s.	−0.3069*	n.s.	0.3720**[a]
$t-4$	n.s.	n.s.	n.s.	−0.2804+	n.s.	0.4552**[a]
$t-5$	n.s.	−0.2830+	n.s.		n.s.	n.s.
1991Q1–1994Q3						
t	n.s.	n.s.	n.s.	n.s.	n.s.	n.s.
$t-1$	n.s.	−0.4026+	n.s.	n.s.	0.7018***	n.s.
$t-2$	−0.4589*	n.s.	−0.4316+	−0.6719***	0.8279***	n.s.
$t-3$	n.s.	n.s.	−0.4277+	−0.5252**	n.s.	n.s.
$t-4$	n.s.	n.s.	−0.5082*	−0.5046*	n.s.	0.4753*
$t-5$	n.s.	n.s.	−0.5009*	n.s.	n.s.	n.s.
1996Q1–2004Q2						
t	−0.5880***	−0.6300***	0.3609**	−0.3656**	0.3155*	n.s.
$t-1$	−0.7082***	−0.6101***	0.2961*	−0.6485***	0.4878***	n.s.
$t-2$	−0.5526***	−0.4201**	0.4066**	−0.5451***	0.4324**	n.s.
$t-3$	−0.4712***	n.s.	n.s.	−0.5719***	0.3753**	n.s.
$t-4$	−0.5580***	n.s.	−0.4192***	−0.5960***	0.2816+	n.s.
$t-5$	n.s.	n.s.	−0.2597+	−0.2675+	n.s.	n.s.

***, **, *, +: significant at 1%, 5%, 10%, 15%.

[a] 1987Q1–1994Q3.

The first column indicates the quarter in which the real exchange rate etc. are measured. Investment and credit are measured as a percentage share of GDP.

All variables have been Hodrick–Prescott detrended.

Table 3.9 Correlation coefficients of Mexican consumption with current and lagged macroeconomic variables

	(1) Real exchange rate I	(2) Real exchange rate II	(3) Real interest rate	(4) Nominal interest rate	(5) Stock market price index	(6) Credit, M2
1986Q1–1994Q3						
t	n.s.	−0.5764***	n.s.	0.3167*	n.s.	0.3863**[a]
t−1	−0.3925**	−0.4233**	n.s.	−0.4381***	n.s.	n.s.
t−2	−0.5112***	−0.4057**	0.2657+[a]	−0.3346**	n.s.	n.s.
t−3	−0.4979***	n.s.	n.s.	−0.3983**	n.s.	n.s.
t−4	−0.4970***	n.s.	n.s.	−0.4372***	n.s.	n.s.
t−5	−0.4846***	n.s.	n.s.		n.s.	n.s.
1991Q1–1994Q3						
t	n.s.	−0.4918*	n.s.	n.s.	n.s.	n.s.
t−1	n.s.	n.s.	n.s.	n.s.	n.s	n.s.
t−2	−0.4570*	n.s.	n.s.	n.s.	n.s.	n.s.
t−3	n.s.	n.s.	n.s.	n.s.	n.s.	n.s.
t−4	n.s.	n.s.	−0.4178+	−0.4276+	0.4821*	n.s.
t−5	n.s.	n.s.	n.s.	n.s.	n.s.	n.s.
1996Q1–2004Q2						
t	−0.3085*	−0.4429***	n.s.	n.s.	n.s.	n.s.
t−1	−0.3440**	−0.4140**	0.3243*	n.s.	n.s.	n.s.
t−2	−0.4683***	−0.4372***	n.s.	−0.3552**	n.s.	n.s.
t−3	−0.5241***	−0.6615***	n.s.	−0.3498**	0.3619**	n.s.
t−4	−0.4010**	−0.4905***	n.s.	−0.3429**	0.3412**	−0.4037**
t−5	−0.4728***	−0.3841**	n.s.	−0.4077**	n.s.	n.s.

***, **, *, +: significant at 1%, 5%, 10%, 15%.
[a] 1987Q1–1994Q3.
The first column indicates the quarter corresponding to the real exchange rate etc.
Consumption and credit are measured as a percentage share of GDP.
Quarterly time effects have been removed from consumption.
All variables have been Hodrick–Prescott detrended.

exchange rate, the nominal and real interest rates, the stock market price index and M2. The results can be summarized in the following terms:

1. The real exchange rate appears to be a very significant determinant of domestic demand, with correlation coefficients above 0.5 and significance levels of 1 per cent. The sign of correlation is negative, implying that depreciations are contractionary, at least in the short run.
2. The interest rate also appears to be a significant determinant of domestic investment and consumption. Note that in the case of consumption the link is definitely stronger when the nominal rather than the real interest rate is considered; for investment, both the nominal and the real interest rate work well.[2]
3. The stock market price index is closely connected with investment across periods; during the band period, when a surge in foreign investment took place, correlation levels were above 0.80. Correlation with consumption is also significant but only from the band period onwards.
4. Finally, M2 appears to be correlated with demand only during the semi-fixed-rate period (although specifically for the band period the evidence is much weaker).

The next step is an examination of the link between capital flows and our group of potential transmission channels (return to Table 3.4). During the semi-fixed-rate period there is a strong, negative correlation between the nominal interest rate and lagged capital flows (column 7). As expected from standard theory, during the floating period the correlation is weaker; perhaps more important, though, is that in the latter period the correlation is *positive* (implying that a rise in the capital inflows, for instance, would lead to a fall in the price of local bonds). Thus, the observed correlation is either spurious or perhaps a reflection of policy actions (a monetary tightening following a capital inflow, for instance).

Unexpectedly, no such link between capital flows and the nominal interest rate can be detected for the band period specifically. The effect can be observed for the *real* interest rate (column 6), during both the band and the floating period. Interestingly, however, the sign of the correlation is positive (meaning a capital inflow is followed by a higher real interest rate). This can reflect the link with the nominal rate for the floating period noted above. However, it can also be explained by the fact that during these two periods, an inflow of capital tended to produce a decline of domestic inflation, a result that probably has to do with the disinflationary role played by the real exchange rate (Ibarra 2003).

The real exchange rate is negatively correlated with (current and lagged) capital flows: as expected, greater inflows lead to real currency appreciation (columns 3 and 4). A comparison of regimes, though, shows that this correlation declined after the shift to a floating regime. This of course is an unexpected finding: the correlation should increase as a counterpart to the observed insulation of the interest rate. What could be the explanation? It should be first noted that the observed response of the *real* exchange rate is based on the link between the *nominal* exchange rate and capital flows: this correlation was strong and very significant during the semi-fixed-exchange-rate period, but null during the floating period (see again Table 3.4, column 5). How can the observed disconnection between the nominal exchange rate and capital flows be explained in the context of a floating regime?

A possible answer can be found in the behaviour of the stock of foreign exchange reserves at the central bank. As shown in Figure 3.1, the quarterly variations in international reserves, at least since the 1980s, have followed closely the evolution of capital flows, which would tend to insulate other macroeconomic variables (such as the exchange rate) from transitory changes in capital flows. However, this link has become particularly tight after the adoption of the floating system.

The more intense use of international reserves for macroeconomic management can be detected through the evolution of the correlation coefficient, which moved from 0.36 during the entire semi-fixed-rate period to 0.63 during the band period and to 0.64 during the float (see Table 3.10). The similarity of coefficients during the band and floating periods could suggest that no major difference in the use of reserves has taken place; however, during the latter period the link is closer on a dollar-by-dollar basis. In particular, the mean absolute value ratio of capital flows to the change in reserves increased from 0.30 to 0.68 across periods.

This closer link between reserves and capital flows has nothing to do with the change in currency regime itself. It can be explained,

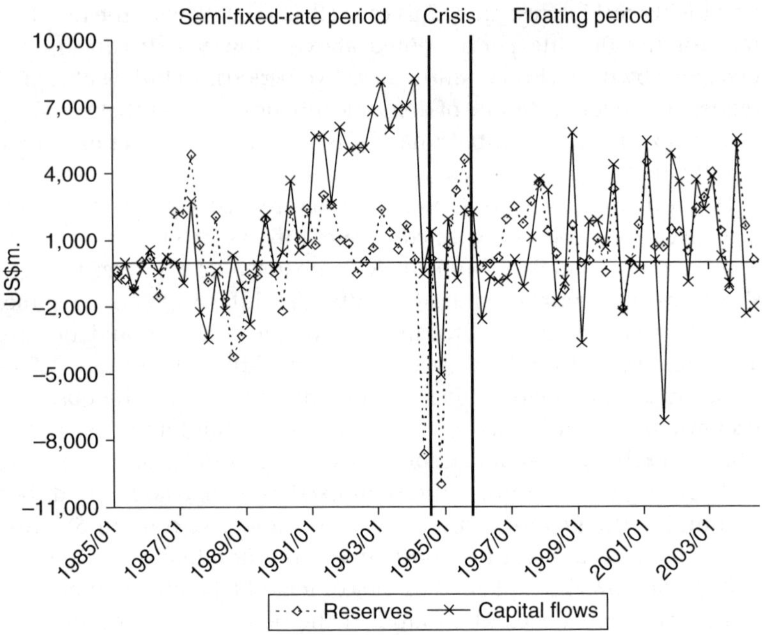

Figure 3.1 Non-FDI flows and variation in international reserves

Table 3.10 Capital flows to Mexico and variation in international reserves

	Correlation coefficient	Mean absolute value		
		(*A*) Capital flows	(*B*) Reserves	Ratio (*B*/*A*)
1986Q1–1994Q3	0.3627**	1156	1583	1.37
1991Q1–1994Q3	0.6317**	5347	1620	0.30
1996Q1–2004Q2	0.6440***	2372	1602	0.68

***, **: significant at 1%, 5%.
Original figures US$m.
Source: Based on data from Banco de Mexico.

instead, by the fact that capital flows were much larger during the band period than under the current system (mean absolute value of $5.3bn per quarter versus only $2.4bn). Naturally, the larger the flow of capital, the more difficult it is to accommodate it through variations in reserves. This is not only because the amount of reserves required to intervene is larger, but also because the sterilization of the change in reserves becomes larger as well. This is particularly costly in a phase of predominantly positive capital inflows – such as during the band period – because sterilization requires that the central bank sells correspondingly large amounts of local currency bonds to the private sector in exchange for foreign currency denominated assets, which entails a cost because of the difference in interest rates.

There has been a slight reduction in the link of M2 with lagged capital flows after the shift to float (see Table 3.4, row 10). But the main change concerns the stock market: the general price index was correlated strongly with lagged capital flows during the semi-fixed-rate period but the link disappeared after the adoption of the new regime (column 9). An important implication is that stock market prices were able to play the role of transmission channel only during the former period; therefore, this is a possible factor in the recently observed disconnection of investment from capital flows.

Why has the role of stock market prices as transmission channel changed? A possible explanation is simply that foreign investment in the Mexican stock market has fallen notably. As we saw already (recall Table 3.1), foreign investment in the stock market rose from only $2.5bn in the late 1980s to more than $26bn in the band period. After this boom, which ended in strong losses for foreign investors because of the devaluation of the peso against the US dollar in late 1994 and early 1995, stock market investments fell dramatically, reaching a cumulative value of only $6.8bn in the entire period of floating. In fact, the correlation coefficient between total capital inflows and investments in the stock market fell from 0.45 in the band period to 0.17 in the floating period (see Table 3.2). The stock market has ceased to be a driving force behind capital flows.

Granger causality tests and transmission channels

The evidence on correlation coefficients is consistent with the view that each of the variables considered (the real exchange rate, the interest rate, the stock market price index and M2) can perform the role of transmission channel for capital flows. This is because they are significantly correlated with lagged capital flows and with future levels of domestic demand. There are, however, changes in the statistical significance of these relationships across the different periods considered in the analysis. In the final part of this chapter we perform a series of Granger causality tests to arrive at firmer conclusions regarding the macroeconomic transmission of capital flows.

The exercise starts from a benchmark equation for either consumption or investment that has on the right-hand side two lags of the corresponding component of domestic demand and of capital flows. Because we want to explore the specific role of each variable in the transmission process, rather than its indirect effect via aggregate output, the benchmark specification also includes lags of the annual GDP growth rate in the set of regressors.

As a next step, in separate equations we include each of the variables that can play a role in the transmission process; the assessment is done by looking at the effect on the *p*-value of the non-causality hypothesis of capital flows on demand and the effect on the size and statistical significance of the coefficients on lagged capital flows. The larger the increase in the *p*-value and the fall in the significance of the lagged capital flow coefficients, the greater is the support for the role of that specific variable as transmission channel.

Estimation of the benchmark equation confirms the previous finding of a recent weakening of the link between investment and capital flows; in particular, it is not possible to reject the hypothesis of non-causality from lagged capital flows to investment during the floating period, irrespective of the number of lags included in the equation, and irrespective of whether the definition of capital flows includes or does not include changes in Mexican assets (see Table 3.11, row 1). Thus, we focus on the semi-fixed period.

It turns out that a significant effect can be found only when changes in Mexican assets are excluded from the measure of capital flows. In the basic specification, the null of non-causality has a relatively low *p*-value of 0.12 (in contrast to 0.65 for the floating period). The sum of statistically significant coefficients for capital flows is 0.25, implying that investment changed by one-quarter of a GDP point for each point of change in capital flows.

We consider first the real exchange rate as a possible transmission channel. It is interesting to note that the conclusion depends on which definition is used. Inclusion of definition I basically does not affect the *p*-value of the non-causality hypothesis nor the significance of the capital flow coefficients (rows 6 and 7). However, if definition II is used (that is, the price ratio between tradables and nontradables),

Table 3.11 Mexico: Granger causality tests, II

	1987Q1–1994Q3		1996Q1–2004Q2	
	Granger test[a]	**Sum of coefficients[b]**	**Granger test[a]**	**Sum of coefficients[b]**
Dependent variable: investment				
Basic specification[c]	0.1178	0.2550**	0.6534	n.s.
With lagged credit, M2	0.0237	0.3523**		
With current credit, M2	0.3805	n.s.		
With lagged stock price index	0.3305	0.2300+		
With current stock price index	0.1191	n.s.		
With lagged real exchange rate I	0.0925	0.2758**		
With current real exchange rate I	0.0858	0.2749**		
With lagged real exchange rate II	0.4106	n.s.		
With current real exchange rate II	0.3145	n.s.		
With lagged real interest rate	0.2791	0.2152+		
With current real interest rate	0.1365	0.2543*		
With lagged nominal interest rate	0.1555	0.2475*		
With current nominal interest rate	0.1060	0.2654**		
Dependent variable: consumption				
Basic specification[d]	0.0164	0.6498**	0.0692	0.9987**
With lagged credit, M2	0.0013	1.4043***	0.0304	1.1349***
With current credit, M2	0.1615	0.5371*	0.3418	n.s.
With lagged stock price index	0.0539	0.7406**	0.1034	0.8811**
With current stock price index	0.1505	0.5811*	0.1049	0.8822**
With lagged real exchange rate I	0.0242	0.5296**	0.0974	0.9575**
With current real exchange rate I	0.0141	0.6379**	0.0352	1.0590***
With lagged real exchange rate II	0.2607	0.4275+	0.3305	n.s.
With current real exchange rate II	0.3664	n.s.	0.2215	n.s.

Continued

Table 3.11 Continued

	1987Q1–1994Q3		1996Q1–2004Q2	
	Granger test[a]	**Sum of coefficients**[b]	**Granger test**[a]	**Sum of coefficients**[b]
With lagged real interest rate	0.0348	0.5766**	0.1084	0.9780**
With current real interest rate	0.0069	1.1297***	0.0771	0.9947*
With lagged nominal interest rate	0.0701	0.5834**	0.1988	0.9147*
With current nominal interest rate	0.0642	0.5430*	0.0541	1.0359**

***, **, *, +: significant at 1%, 5%, 10% and 15% respectively.
[a] *p*-value for the hypothesis: all coefficients on lagged capital flows are equal to zero.
[b] Only those with *p*-values below 0.15.
[c] RHS variables: constant, two lags of investment, two lags of GDP growth rate, two lags of capital flows (excluding Mexican assets).
[d] RHS variables: constant, two lags of consumption, two lags of GDP growth rate, two lags of capital flows.
For the period 1996Q1–2004Q2, it includes the current value and one lag of GDP growth rate (instead of two lags).
All variables have been Hodrick–Prescott detrended, and quarterly time effects removed from consumption.
Capital flows, domestic demand and credit are expressed as percentages of GDP.

then the *p*-value jumps to more than 0.3 and the capital flow coefficients become non-significant (rows 8 and 9). The interpretation is that the real exchange rate, understood in the second sense, performed an important role as transmission channel during the semi-fixed period.

Similar conclusions are obtained for credit (M2) and the stock market price index (rows 3 to 4). In contrast, the results are weaker for the (real and nominal) interest rate: its inclusion in the regression equations increases the *p*-value for the acceptance of the hypothesis of non-causality (particularly when lagged values are included), but the coefficients on capital flows remain statistically different from zero (and their size not much below that obtained in the benchmark specification) at the 10 per cent or 15 per cent significance level.

The evidence on the causality of capital flows on demand during the semi-fixed-rate period is stronger for consumption than for investment. In the benchmark specification, the non-causality hypothesis from lagged capital flows can be rejected at 5 per cent, and the sum of coefficients is a much higher 0.65 (row 14). Thus, consumption tended to increase in more than half a point for each point of rise in capital flows. The evidence on causality persists during the floating period: although the *p*-value for the non-causality hypothesis rose to 0.07 (from 0.02), the coefficients on lagged capital flows remained significant at 5 per cent and there was a rise in their size, from 0.65 to 0.99.

Focusing on the transmission during the semi-fixed-rate period, we see that the strongest evidence is again for the real exchange rate (definition II; rows 21 and 22). In this case we have both non-significant capital flow coefficients and the highest rise in the *p*-value for the non-causality hypothesis among all possible transmission channels. Next in significance are credit and stock market prices, which raise the *p*-value of the non-causality hypothesis to 0.16 and 0.15, respectively. In both cases it is mainly the current value of the third variables that is significant: this is again consistent with the idea that capital flows affect the third variable with a lag, which then is transmitted to consumption demand (recall from the correlation coefficients in Table 3.6 that indeed a significant link of capital flows with credit and stock market prices surfaced only after a number of lags).

Similarly to what we observed in the case of investment, the weakest evidence concerns the interest rate. The inclusion of this variable (in real or nominal terms) leaves the *p*-value for non-causality always below 0.10, while the reduction in the size of the capital flow coefficients is minimal. Thus, during the semi-fixed-rate period it was the real exchange rate, stock prices and M2 that performed the main role as transmission channels for capital flows; the possible role of the interest rate was comparatively small.

Most of these results carry over to the consumption equation in the floating period. The real exchange rate (again, definition II) persists as a strong transmission channel, raising the *p*-value of the non-causality hypothesis from capital flows to consumption to 0.33 (from 0.07 in the benchmark specification; see rows 14 and 21). The inclusion of the nominal interest rate also raises the *p*-value, but only to 0.20 (and the capital flow coefficients remain statistically significant; see row 25). It can be noticed that these effects are stronger using the nominal rather than the real rate. Somewhat unexpectedly, M2 appears as a significant transmission channel, even more clearly so than during the semi-fixed-rate period (row 16); this is surprising given the lack of positive correlation between M2 and domestic demand observed for the floating period (see again Table 3.9).

The greatest change is that in the floating period the stock market price index ceased to be a significant channel for capital flows. In particular, the *p*-value for the non-causality hypothesis increases from 0.07 in the basic specification, to only 0.10 in the regression including the (current or lagged) index of stock market prices; moreover, the statistical significance of the capital flow coefficients basically does not change, while their size falls from 0.99 to 0.88.

Summary

The purpose of this chapter has been to describe the recent evolution of capital flows to Mexico – with a focus on non-FDI flows – and to analyse their macroeconomic effects. The relative importance of non-FDI flows has varied over time: after the drought years brought about by the 1982 debt crisis, there was a boom in portfolio investment during the early 1990s. Then, as the country moved from a semi-fixed exchange rate system to a floating regime, there was a significant reduction in cumulative flows. Even in the most recent period, though, non-FDI flows have remained a significant source of macroeconomic shocks because of their large volatility levels.

We have found that investment and consumption demand were significantly correlated with *lagged* capital flows during the semi-fixed-rate period, but that only consumption remained linked during the floating period. Capital flows appear to follow a pro-cyclical pattern, in the sense that they respond positively to changes in income and investment demand, although there is some evidence of anti-cyclicality with respect to consumption during the floating period. This pro-cyclical behaviour can be reinforced by bandwagon-type effects mediated by the real exchange rate: a currency appreciation, for instance, leads to greater demand and inflows. But greater inflows tend to appreciate the currency, which feeds further into capital inflows.

Credit levels (as measured by M2) and more importantly the real exchange rate (defined as the price ratio between tradables and nontradables) have played a significant role as transmission channels from capital flows to domestic demand; in contrast, the evidence is weak for the interest rate. This description applies to consumption across periods, and to investment during the semi-fixed-rate period.

The real exchange rate has continued to play an important role, even though there has been a purposeful use of international reserves to match the short-term fluctuations of capital flows that has resulted in a weakening of the link of the latter with both the interest rate and the exchange rate.

Domestic investment has become largely detached from capital flows during the floating period. One possible explanation is that during this period foreign investment in the Mexican stock market has been small, and as a consequence stock market prices have ceased to respond to variations in capital flows. This may have helped to break the nexus between investment and capital flows but, just as in the case of the use of international reserves as an insulation device, it is not a virtue to be attributed directly to the floating regime itself.

Appendix: data definitions and sources

Capital flows, domestic demand – investment and consumption – and credit – M2 – are expressed as shares of GDP for the estimation of correlation coefficients and Granger regressions. For demand and credit, nominal values in pesos were used. For capital flows, the Mexican GDP was first expressed in US dollars using the current value of the nominal exchange rate. All variables in this analysis were Hodrick–Prescott-detrended and quarterly effects were removed from the series for consumption and GDP. GDP was expressed in natural logarithms.

Capital flows. Corresponds to the capital account balance less net FDI. Original data in millions of US dollars. Source: Banco de Mexico, Balance of Payments data.

Investment, Consumption and GDP. Original data in billions of pesos. Source: National Institute of Statistics (INEGI), National Accounts System data.

Real exchange rate I. Consumer price ratio between the US and Mexico. US dollar prices were expressed in Mexican pesos using the current value of the nominal exchange rate. Source: Banco de Mexico and US Bureau of Labor Statistics.

Real exchange rate II. Domestic price ratio between tradables and nontradables. Tradable prices were approximated by the index of implicit prices of the manufacturing sector, while nontradables correspond to the construction sector. Source: National Institute of Statistics (INEGI), National Accounts System data.

Nominal exchange rate. Wholesale rate, period average. Source: Banco de Mexico.

Nominal interest rate. Annualized 28-day Treasury bill (cete) rate, average from weekly auctions. Source: Banco de Mexico.

Real interest rate. Nominal interest rate less current inflation. Inflation was calculated as the annual (Q/Q) percentage variation in the consumer price index published by the Banco de Mexico.

Stock market price index. Average of the maximum and minimum values of the overall price index of the Mexican stock exchange for each month, divided by the consumer price index. Source: Bolsa Mexicana de Valores.

M2. Source and definition: Banco de Mexico.

Acknowledgements

For their comments and suggestions, I would like to thank participants at the International Conference on Emerging Markets, held at the Westminster Business School, University of Westminster, 10–12 June 2004. Financial support from CONACYT is gratefully acknowledged.

Notes

1. Actually, the floating system was adopted in the final days of December 1994, in the midst of a currency run. Financial and macroeconomic instability persisted during 1995. We leave aside from the analysis the observations corresponding to the last quarter of 1994 and the whole of 1995, on the assumption that the crisis period may present some exceptional patterns that in fact are not representative of the working of the floating system under more normal circumstances.
2. Except for the positive sign of the correlation coefficients for the first lags of the floating period. This shift in the sign of correlations – which also can be observed in the case of consumption – may have to do with the difficulties to estimate a meaningful value for the real interest rate under conditions of high and unstable inflation.

References

Furman, J. and J.E. Stiglitz (1998) *Economic Crises: Evidence and Insights from East Asia*, Brookings Papers on Economic Activity no 2. Washington, DC: Brookings Institution, pp. 1–135.

Galindo, A. and A. Izquierdo (2003) *Sudden Stops and Exchange Rate Strategies in Latin America*, Inter-American Development Bank Working Paper no. 484, Washington, DC. February.

Gavin, M., R. Hausmann and L. Leiderman (1996) 'The Macroeconomics of Capital Flows to Latin America: Experience and Policy Issues', in Hausmann, R.

and L. Rojas-Suárez (eds), *Volatile Capital Flows. Taming Their Impact on Latin America*. Inter-American Development Bank, Washington, DC, pp. 1–40.

Ibarra, C.A. (2003) 'Slow Growth, Trade Liberalization and the Mexican Disease: A Medium-Term Macroeconomic Model with an Application to Mexico', *International Review of Applied Economics*, 17(3), 269–92.

Iwata, S. and E. Tanner (2003) *Pick Your Poison: The Exchange Rate Regime and Capital Account Volatility in Emerging Markets*, IMF Working Paper no. 03/92, Washington, DC.

Lustig, N. and J. Ros (1999) 'Economic reforms, stabilization policies and the "Mexican disease" ', in Taylor (ed.), *After Neoliberalism*. University of Michigan Press.

Mattar, J., J.C. Moreno-Brid and W. Peres (2002) *Foreign Investment in Mexico after Economic Reform*, ECLAC Estudios y Perspectivas 10, July.

Montiel, P. and C.M. Reinhart (2001) 'The Dynamics of Capital Movements to Emerging Economies During the 1990s', in Griffith-Jones, S., M.F. Montes and A. Nasution, (eds), *Short-term Capital Flows and Economic Crises*, UNU/WIDER Studies in Development Economics. Oxford University Press.

Ocampo, J.A. (2000) *Developing Countries' Anti-cyclical Policies in a Globalized World*, ECLAC United Nations, Temas de Coyuntura Series no. 13, November.

Prasad, E., K. Rogoff, S.J. Wei and M.A. Kose (2003) *Effects of Financial Globalization on Developing Countries: Some Empirical Evidence*. International Monetary Fund, Washington, DC, March.

Schwartz, M.J. (1994) 'Exchange Rate Bands and Monetary Policy: The Case of Mexico' *Economía Mexicana*, 3(2), 287–317.

Svensson, L.E.O. (1992) 'An Interpretation of Recent Research on Exchange Rate Target Zones', *Journal of Economic Perspectives*', 6(4), 119–144.

Trigueros, I. (1998) 'Capital Inflows and Investment Performance: Mexico', in French-R.F., Davis and H. Reisen (eds), *Capital Flows and Investment Performance. Lessons from Latin America*. ECLAC and OECD Development Centre Studies, Paris, pp. 193–214.

4

'Blind Bargaining' and the Effects of Foreign Direct Investment on Recipient States: The Case of Post-Soviet and Eastern European Countries

Nataliya Ass and Matthias Beck

Introduction

In recent years foreign direct investment (FDI) has become increasingly important for transition and developing economies. This emphasis on FDI is closely related to the ongoing globalization of world economic processes and the concomitant increase in international capital flows. Among transition economies, in particular, there is belief that the process of building a compatible economic infrastructure requires mobilization not only of national resources but also of the involvement of investment sources which are situated beyond the borders of the domestic economy (Lazebnyk 1997:84). In this context, large-scale diversified international investment activity has often been considered as one of the main leverages for the long-term development of a highly integrated economy (Zaxarin 2000:88–89). Recipient states with positive attitudes towards FDI typically expect that the utilization of foreign investment will provide them with access to contemporary technologies and management, contribute to the creation of national investment markets, increase the efficiency of both production factors and goods markets, maintain macroeconomic stabilization and facilitate the solution of social problems which might have arisen during the transitional period (Maxmudov 1998:39–40).

Moran identifies these assumptions with regard to FDI in transition economies as the 'benign model' of FDI and development. In accordance with this model, the host country expects that 'under reasonably competitive conditions FDI should raise efficiency, expand output, and lead to higher economic growth in the country' (Moran 1998:19–20). Moreover, the model emphasizes the fact that

> the additional supply of capital should lower the relative return to capital, while the additional demand for labour should bid up the wages of workers, thereby equalizing the distribution of income and improving (quite probably) health and education throughout society. (Moran 1998:20)

In recent years, some empirical research has argued that 'FDI is not necessarily an indication of good health for an economy; to the contrary, riskier countries with less developed financial markets and weak institutions tend to attract less capital, but more in the form of FDI' (Elo 2003:3). Hausmann and Fernandez-Arias (2000), for instance, suggest that the proposition 'that capital inflows tend to take the form of FDI – share of FDI in total liabilities tends to be higher – in countries that are safer, more promising and with better institutions and policies' (Hausmann and Fernandez-Arias 2003:3) is misleading. They find that, while capital flows tend to go to countries that are safer, more developed, more open, more stable and have better and advanced institutions and financial markets, the share of FDI in total capital flows to these countries tends to be lower than the share of other forms of capital flows. Implied in this analysis is the view that FDI is not necessarily an indication of good health; rather countries that are riskier, poorer, more volatile and more closed, less financially developed with weaker institutions and with more natural resources, tend to attract a greater share of capital in the form of FDI (ibid.:3, 12).

It can be argued that, contrary to the anticipations of host states that FDI will always improve economic welfare as a result of the attraction of 'benign' FDI,[1] it is often 'malign' FDI[2] that targets the unstable transition and developing countries, with high levels of country risk and political instability, which are often experiencing a lack of progress in the implementation of structural reforms.

According to Moran's 'malign model' of FDI and development:

> instead of filling the gap between savings and investment, Multinational Enterprises (MNEs) may lower domestic savings and investment by extracting rents and siphoning off the capital through preferred access to local capital markets and local supplies of foreign exchange. Instead of closing the gap between investment and foreign exchange, they might drive domestic producers out of business and substitute imported inputs. The MNE may reinvest in the same or related industries in the host country and extend its market power. The repatriation of profits might drain capital from the host country. MNEs' use of 'inappropriate' capital intensive technologies may produce a small labour elite while consigning many workers to the ranks of the unemployed. Their tight control over technology, higher management functions and export channels may prevent the beneficial spillovers and externalities hoped for in more optimistic scenarios. (Moran 1998:21)

Further to this, it can be argued that the neo-patrimonial nature of rule in some states, in particular post-Soviet ones, stipulates the presence of a 'blind-bargaining' element in the relationships between MNEs and these states. 'Blind bargaining', reflecting latent conflict between genuine economic goals and the private interests of the state ruling elite, creates high levels of uncertainty and instability with regard to bargaining outcomes. The higher levels of uncertainty and unpredictability which result from the personalization of power and decision-making in these states, in turn, are likely to encourage MNEs either to disengage themselves from the respective territory, or to seek conditions which are excessively biased in their favour. 'Blind bargaining' can be considered as one of the explanations for the failure of post-Soviet states in attracting good-quality or 'benign' FDI. Following Hausmann and Fernandez-Arias (2000) and Elo (2003) it can be argued that the risky investment profile of these countries is likely to lead to a situation where a greater share of FDI is 'malign'. This means that investment either does not contribute to the host states' growth, or even influences negatively the overall development of the host state.

A comparative analysis of the relationship between the volumes of FDI inflows and recipient country's indicators is applied in a test of five different groupings of countries:

1. all CEE including post-Soviet states, the Baltic states, Central European accession and non-accession countries;
2. all post-Soviet states except the Baltic states;
3. Central European accession and non-accession countries and the Baltic states;
4. Central European post-Soviet states including Belarus, Moldova, Russia and Ukraine;
5. Central Asian states.

The indicators considered are: the overall country risk, political, economic, legal, tax, operational and security risks, inflation, unemployment, GDP per capita, export per capita, trade balance and hosts' debt as share of GDP. The test showed that the ability to attract FDI and quality of the attracted inflows corresponds with indicators of stability in a country. Moreover, it was detected that FDI as a percentage of GDP, for some groups of countries, is negatively related to GDP per capita, which can be seen as an indication that FDI is likely to shrink once a certain level of prosperity is reached in a country. For certain groups of countries, mainly post-Soviet states, significant positive correlations between FDI and debt and negative correlations between FDI and trade balance can be also observed. The inference that these states mainly attract 'malign' FDI can be owing to the fact that FDI impacts negatively on the trade balance of these recipient states.

FDI performance versus FDI potential

The role of FDI has grown dramatically in transition economies during recent years. Between 1983 and 1988, FDI volumes grew at 20 per cent annually in real terms, while world trade volumes grew only at a compound annual rate of 5 per cent (Vernon 1971:14). Over the course of the 1990s, FDI volumes rose from US$24bn per year in 1990 to approximately US$120bn per year by the beginning of 1998. Private capital flows totalled more than four-fifths of all capital inflows to less-developed countries and countries in transition in 1998. Among these capital inflows FDI was, and stays, the largest and most stable source of capital, climbing in recent years to nearly 50 per cent (Moran 1998:15).

In 2000, FDI grew by 18 per cent, faster than other economic aggregates like world production, capital formation and trade, reaching a record US$1.3tn (UNCTAD 2001:1). This growth was disrupted by a sharp 41 per cent fall in FDI inflows in 2001 and even further by a 20 per cent (or US$651bn) decline in 2002, which was attributable primarily to weak economic growth in the world (UNCTAD 2003:xiii, 1).

Interestingly, the decline in FDI in 2002 was uneven across regions and countries with Central and Eastern Europe (CEE) being among a small group of countries which resisted the negative trend in FDI performance. Thus, while flows to developed and developing countries each fell by 22 per cent (to US$460bn and US$162bn, respectively), flows into the CEE region increased on average by 15 per cent, with amounts of FDI inflows increasing in 9 countries and falling in 10 countries of the region (UNCTAD 2003:3). The increase of investment flows into CEE countries was accompanied by a parallel 70 per cent rise of FDI inflows into the primary sector and a decline into the manufacturing and services sectors (ibid.). Specifically, FDI rose in mining, quarrying and petroleum, while being severely affected in finance, transport, storage and communications and virtually unchanged in health and social services (UNCTAD 2003:5).

The same time period saw takeovers of Transgas by German RWE, and Slovensky Plynarensky Priemisel by Gazprom, in the Czech Republic and Slovakia, respectively, all of which contributed significantly to the growth of FDI in CEE. Russian Yukos, meanwhile, acquired the Lithuanian company Mazeikiu Nafta and the Slovakian company Traspetrol, and Eurochem acquired the Lithuanian chemical firm Lifosa. A total of 60 per cent of the Russian investment targeting Ukraine (Russia's favourite host destination within the Commonwealth of Independent States or CIS) as also aimed at the energy sector, specifically by Gazprom and Zarubezhneft, though this was followed by investment in the machinery project 'Sylovye Mashini' (UNCTAD 2003:60–61).

Azerbaijan also experienced a significant increase in FDI in 2002, with investment growing by more than 500 per cent in comparison with the previous year. Belarus, Armenia and Georgia, meanwhile, experienced FDI growth relative to the previous year as well (see Table 4.1).

UNCTAD's inward FDI performance index and its inward FDI potential index provide a comprehensive enough and interesting

Table 4.1 Foreign direct investment inflows into Central and Eastern Europe and Central Asia ($m)

Country	Year					
	1997	1998	1999	2000	2001	2002
1. Former USSR countries						
1.1 Central and Eastern Europe						
1. Belarus	352	203	444	119	96	227
2. Moldova	79	76	38	129	156	111
3. Russia	4,865	2,761	3,309	2,714	2,469	2,421
4. Ukraine	623	743	496	595	792	693
1.2 Central Asia						
5. Armenia	52	221	122	104	70	100
6. Azerbaijan	1,115	1,023	510	129	227	1,067
7. Georgia	243	265	82	131	110	146
8. Kazakhstan	1,321	1,152	1,472	1,283	2,823	2,561
9. Kyrgyzstan	84	109	44	−2	5	−12
10. Tajikistan	18	25	21	22	9	9
11. Turkmenistan	108	62	89	131	150	100
12. Uzbekistan	167	140	121	73	570	65
1.3 Baltic countries/ EU accession countries						
13. Estonia	267	581	305	387	542	307
14. Latvia	521	357	347	410	164	396
15. Lithuania	355	926	486	379	446	732
2. Central and Eastern Europe						
2.1 EU accession countries						
16. Bulgaria	505	537	819	1002	813	479
17. Czech Rep.	1,286	3,700	6,310	4,984	5,639	9,319
18. Hungary	2,167	2,037	1,977	1,646	2,440	854
19. Poland	4,908	6,365	7,270	9,341	5,713	4,119
20. Romania	1,215	2,031	1,041	1,025	1,157	1,106
21. Slovakia	220	684	390	1,925	1,579	4,012
22. Slovenia	334	216	107	136	503	1,865
2.2 Other countries						
23. Albania	48	45	41	143	207	213
24. Bosnia and Herzegovina	1	56	154	147	130	321
25. Croatia	533	932	1,467	1,089	1,561	981
26. Macedonia (TFYR)	16	118	32	177	442	77
27. Serbia and Montenegro	740	113	112	25	165	475

Source: UNCTAD (2003).

picture of the patterns and trends in changes of the post-Soviet states' performance regarding their success in attracting FDI (see Table 4.2). The inward FDI performance index, calculated as a ratio of the country's share in global FDI inflows to its share in global GDP, ranks countries by FDI relative to their economic size, while the inward FDI potential index captures several factors (apart from market size).[3]

An analysis of these indices for the post-Soviet, Baltic and CEE accession as well as non-accession countries reveals several distinct patterns of regional performance. Not surprisingly, the data on CEE accession, as well as other non-ex-Soviet states, and Baltic countries indicates that significant progress was made during the transition period 1990–2001 both in terms of improving their performance and in terms of increasing their potential for attracting FDI to their markets. Apart from Hungary and the Czech Republic, all of these countries were poor economic performers, possessing relatively low initial potential in comparison with Eastern European ex-Soviet states. Yet all of them managed to progress significantly, which is reflected in data on FDI inflows.

Bulgaria, for instance, which ranked 103rd out of 140 economies assessed in terms of its performance for the period 1990–2, managed to move to 25th position in 1999–2001, though it was downgraded in terms of its potential from 42nd to 64th place. The opposite situation could be observed for Hungary. From being initially ranked 16th in terms of performance and 63rd in terms of potential, the country moved into the category of 'underperforming economies', being allocated 53rd position for performance and 41st for potential in 1999–2001.[4] Though still slightly underperforming, Poland was upgraded in terms of both performance and potential from 81st and 59th to 47th and 43rd, respectively.

Ranked as relatively high potential in 1990–2, Belarus at 28th, Moldova at 35th, Ukraine at 49th and Russia at 33rd all (except for Russia, downgraded just to the 35th place) dropped to much lower levels in 1999–2001. Belarus moved to the 63rd position, Moldova to 109th and Ukraine to 85th. Interestingly (especially taking into consideration Moldova's very low potential), out of all these significantly underperforming economies, Moldova was among the leaders within the category of above-performers. The performance index ranked it 13th in 1990–2 and slightly dropped in 1999–2001, moving the country to the still very advanced 19th place. Ukraine's performance deteriorated to a much greater extent in late 1990s, with the country

Table 4.2 Inward FDI performance (PeI) and potential (PoI) indices rankings, 1990–2001 (three-year moving average)

	1990–2		1991–3		1992–4		1993–5		1995–6		1995–7		1996–8		1997–9		1998–2000		1999–2001	
Country	PeI	PoI	PeI	PoI	PeI	PoI	PeI	PoI	PeI	PoI	PeI	PoI	PeI	PoI	PeI	PoI	PeI	PoI	PeI	PoI
1. Former USSR Countries																				
1.1 Central and Eastern Europe																				
Belarus	124	28	122	32	112	31	119	71	113	72	92	66	94	68	77	68	92	64	87	63
Moldova	13	35	21	36	38	40	35	46	45	96	36	98	49	107	48	120	29	125	18	109
Russia	120	33	109	33	109	35	108	34	107	36	104	36	110	37	107	36	105	35	108	35
Ukraine	61	49	71	65	86	67	97	64	98	75	96	79	99	84	96	86	98	88	88	85
1.2 Central Asia																				
Armenia	27	127	74	131	114	120	102	116	99	127	79	123	22	129	19	125	19	126	38	118
Azerbaijan	...	...	...	...	116	134	28	131	4	133	1	130	1	130	1	131	10	118	33	106
Georgia	...	...	...	...	122	129	121	133	89	137	35	137	25	137	26	136	38	135	63	131
Kazakhstan	89	61	24	75	30	85	17	92	21	98	17	97	23	96	24	97	23	93	15	83
Kyrgyzstan	...	...	96	126	47	133	23	134	24	134	23	134	33	132	33	132	67	130	107	128
Tajikistan	90	105	81	116	81	119	59	103	63	116	68	121	82	136	88	137	93	137	93	136
Turkmenistan	...	...	...	...	...	...	...	...	...	...	...	...	...	...	...	...	...	...	...	...
Uzbekistan	123	56	106	59	74	52	104	72	110	94	110	95	107	101	103	100	108	97	84	95
1.3 Baltic countries/ EU accession countries																				
Estonia	59	76	29	90	19	83	15	65	23	60	24	55	14	47	16	40	18	39	21	38
Latvia	62	43	42	6	17	89	20	87	13	91	11	86	13	71	23	66	33	63	51	55
Lithuania	107	70	77	91	80	92	80	89	68	85	51	81	27	61	27	60	34	61	60	56

2. Central and Eastern Europe																				
2.1 EU accession countries																				
Bulgaria	103	42	89	53	89	60	95	48	86	59	60	74	44	58	30	63	27	68	25	64
Czech Rep.	40	58	30	50	32	48	30	39	30	40	40	40	37	40	22	39	15	38	11	37
Hungary	16	63	8	63	15	63	8	57	10	54	13	54	32	48	44	45	53	45	53	41
Poland	81	59	62	57	50	56	42	54	40	53	45	53	46	41	45	43	42	43	47	43
Romania	109	85	103	93	85	97	84	88	83	89	69	101	52	97	52	101	64	98	75	91
Slovakia	71	62	65	62	61	61	56	47	64	48	86	48	79	49	84	49	41	49	26	48
Slovenia	83	89	70	78	76	69	88	43	94	42	93	43	101	30	108	30	112	30	105	29
2.2 Other countries																				
Albania	77	123	27	121	22	118	29	123	35	120	49	131	69	124	99	109	88	103	67	97
Bosnia and Herzegovina	…	…	…	…	…	…	…	…	…	…	…	…	…	…	…	…	…	…	…	…
Croatia	…	…	94	117	84	016	89	82	69	80	64	77	50	57	38	53	30	31	22	46
Macedonia (TFYR)	…	…	…	…	104	110	111	104	116	112	128	109	102	110	97	105	73	101	29	102
Serbia and Montenegro	…	…	…	…	…	…	…	…	…	…	…	…	…	…	…	…	…	…	…	…

Rating out of 140 countries.

Source: UNCTAD (2003).

being downgraded from 61st to 88th place. Russia and Belarus, though having a much lower initial performance index in the early 1990s (120th and 124th, respectively) showed insignificant but consistent progress during this first decade of their transition to a market, moving to 108th and 87th places, respectively.

The Central Asian countries, by contrast, all had very low potential for attracting FDI flows and were marginally better in their performance on FDI attraction than was indicated by their potential index. Azerbaijan was the most extraordinary example of performance above expectations. With high levels of natural resource endowment, Azerbaijan, being ranked in terms of its potential between 130th and 133rd (out of 140 economies) during 1995–9, was ranked highest in terms of FDI inflows. Kazakhstan and Kyrgyzstan are also good examples of the preferential attractiveness of natural resources to foreign investors. Being ranked 97th and 134th by their potential index in 1995–7, they occupied 17th and 23rd positions, respectively, in terms of their performance.

These data indicate that, in spite of high levels of economic and political instability, foreign investors tend to be attracted to underdeveloped transition countries with high levels of resource endowments. However, statistics show that despite some success of transition economies in attracting FDI, developed countries still remain the prime destination of FDI, accounting for more than three-quarters of global inflows. Thus, inflows to developed countries increased by 21 per cent and amounted to a little over US$1tn, while FDI inflows to developing countries, though also growing, reached only US$240bn. CEE countries in Central and Eastern Europe maintained their share of 2 per cent in 2000, with inflows of US$27bn (UNCTAD 2001:1).

The following sections will investigate the potential reasons for the degradation of post-Soviet states in terms of their potential attractiveness for FDI and the existing imbalance of investment allocations among transition countries.

The reality of the post-Soviet investment environment

One of the most threatening problems for post-Soviet states arises not from the maladaption of production, enterprises, branches as such but from the existence of structural barriers. These barriers arise, inter alia, from an inconsistency of technologies, a low capability for investment and innovation, and a lack of institutional and social capacity (Cornia and Popov 2001:270).

Despite examples of several successful investment projects in some post-Soviet states, the disadvantages and uncertainties of investing in these countries outweigh the potential benefits. Among the major factors which deter foreign investors are negative international rating of these hosts, lack of state responsibility, omnipresence of vested interests, high levels of risks (political and economic, in particular), lack of stability in legislation (including contradictory and insufficiently transparent legislation) and its implementation, weak court systems, corruption infringement of investor rights, infringement of intellectual property rights, long and unclear procedures of investment registration, breaches of agreements and contracts by representatives of official state organizations and private enterprises, imperfect state guarantees for foreign investors and unattractive tax systems (often with high taxes and the subjective interpretation of active laws), and an undeveloped infrastructure (Gudkevych 2001:57; Yacheistova 2001:11–13).

One of the main concerns for foreign investors in post-Soviet states is the vagueness of government attitudes to foreign investment. These attitudes often differ across government branches and change with regime shifts. However, officially most post-Soviet states profess their commitment to supporting FDI.

Today, the unequal regional distribution of FDI in the post-Soviet territories is determined primarily by the presence of natural resources and, secondarily, by the attitudes of regional authorities towards FDI. Accordingly it has been argued that in Russia attitudes of '89 regional governments vary greatly and often depend on the personality of the regional governor' (WMRC 2004h:52); for example:

> The liberal political leadership of Nignii Novgorod has been highly encouraging for FDI, while the elites of other regions, say Volgograd, which is still run by an old-style communist administration, have been hostile, particularly when it harms their own business interests. (Ibid.)

As a result,

> FDI are now mostly concentrated in the big industrial towns and regions as Moscow, St. Petersburg, Nignii Novgorod; a big share

> of FDI is accumulated in central and north regions of Russia, in particular in Leningradskaya, Novgorodskaya, Kostromskaya oblast. In Tatarstan, regional authorities also managed to create attractive conditions for foreign investments. (Yacheistova 2001: 11–12)

These problems are accompanied by an uneven sectoral distribution of FDI. Hitherto, natural resource and food industries have been the most attractive targets for foreign investment. In Russia, the fuel and food sectors lead in terms of share of total FDI inflows with 23 per cent and 28 per cent, respectively. They are followed by trade, transport and telecommunications. The machinery, timber and other sectors, meanwhile, hardly receive any investment at all. Large-scale investments in oil and gas sectors have included about 50 joint ventures, involving American, British, French, German, Canadian, Japanese and other companies. The scale of projects in the food sector is significant as well. Foreign companies have shown interest in pastries and meat industries, production of non-alcohol drinks, beer and tobacco (ibid.).

Since its independence, Ukraine has attracted less than US$6bn in FDI, which comprises only about a seventh of the officially estimated US$40bn required for restructuring the Ukrainian economy. A detailed analysis of FDI flows indicates that they are quite small and often used inefficiently. For example, foreign investment inflows in Ukraine during the first half of the year 2001 were 12.4 per cent less then the amount of FDI inflows during the corresponding period of the year 2000. As in Russia, foreign investors targeted the Ukrainian food and agricultural processing industry. Of the total investment inflows into this sector the FDI share comprised 19.8 per cent. Wholesale and sale mediation attracted 13.9 per cent of investment. Investments in the machine-building industry, financial sectors and transport were equal to 8.2 per cent, 7.9 per cent and 6.8 per cent of total investment inflows, respectively.

Not every Ukrainian region is favoured to the same extent by the volumes of foreign investment inflows. The capital, Kyiv, is in the most favourable position, followed by the Kyiv region with the high level of investment growth. In terms of FDI attractiveness the resource-rich Donetskyi and Poltavskyi regions, and the preferentially geographically located Odeskyi region, have also had significant success (State Statistics Committee of Ukraine 1996–2002).

Despite official encouragement of FDI, many potential foreign investors have been discouraged from investing in Ukraine because of changing privatization rules and the capricious ways in which some investors have been treated. One example of this is that while one investment law guarantees foreign investors equal treatment with local companies and possible privileges, other legislation restricts foreign ownership in certain sectors (WMRC 2004i:44).

In Moldova, actions by the communist government with regard to foreign investment have led World Bank experts to reprimand the country and warn it against practising expropriation. Subsequent fears that agriculture could be recollectivized have hindered further investment in the agricultural sector. As a result, Moldova has attracted less than US$50m. since independence. In monetary terms Russia is now the largest foreign investor to Moldova, providing 36 per cent of FDI, almost all of which is accounted for by Gazprom's gas utilities and the Lukoil joint venture (WMRC 2004f:30).

Similarly, in Turkmenistan the largest share of FDI has been received by the gas sector. Although the legal framework for FDI in the extractive sector is very detailed, there is no guarantee that the contract will not be re-examined by authorities. Thus, it has been argued that Turkmen authorities are favourable to foreign investors only to the extent that they control them (WMRC 2004h:21).

Azerbaijan holds a leading position among post-Soviet states in terms of volumes of FDI inflows. The largest share of FDI is received by the country's main industry – oil – despite raising the frictions between the vested interests of certain state authorities and investors in this sector. In contrast, some other industries are much more sensitive to corruption and instability in this country. For instance, as a result of high levels of corruption, unfair practices by officials and declining traffic volumes, foreign airlines were forced to abandon their operations in the country. During the period 1999–2000, six different companies, namely Austrian Airlines, British Airways, Emirates, KLM, Lufthansa and Pakistan Air have ceased operations in Baku's Bina International Airport (WMRC 2004a:34).

In Kazakhstan, which received US$17bn in FDI since independence, even 'official' attitudes to foreign investment have deteriorated. A number of high-profile international investors, such as TengizChevroil, Canada's Hurricane Hydrocarbons Ltd and the Carachaganak Petroleum

Operating Company, have faced Environment Ministry accusations of opaque sales, environmental breaches and preference for the hiring of more local contractors. Moreover, a newly enacted investment law, approved in 2003, stipulates that new contracts negotiated with foreign companies will not contain a 'grandfather clause' that shields the company from regulatory and tax changes. The law also prevents companies from resorting to international arbitration if the Kazakh government forbids this. Furthermore, the law eliminates preferences for foreign investors, 'creating a level playing field between domestic and foreign companies' (WMRC 2004d:39).

In Belarus, there have also been an alarmingly large number of pullouts by foreign investors. Here, the reactionary and capricious attitude of President Alyaksandr Lukashenka acts as a potent deterrent for investors. The failure to agree terms with authorities, following lengthy discussions, resulted in the withdrawal of the furniture-maker IKEA from Belarus where it had planned to invest US$25m. in a sawmill in August 2002. In July 2003, the German investor MAN Nutzfahrzeug pulled out of its 1997 truck-manufacturing and semi-tractor joint venture with the Minsk Motor Factory (MAZ), with the MAZ deputy director suggesting that the Germans had failed to take into account 'the unique style of management that exists in Belarusian industry' (WMRC 2004b:27).

Kyrgyzstan, lastly, markets itself as an 'oasis of stability in an uncertain region – "the Switzerland of Central Asia" ' (WMRC 2004e:26). Though operational impediments to foreign investment have not yet been eradicated in the country, both official and public attitudes towards FDI seem to be positive. By 2003 total FDI flows to the country reached US$116m. Yet FDI in Kyrgyzstan is mainly concentrated in the gold-mining sector, which has led to an unequal regional distribution of capital flows, as in case of all other post-Soviet states, with, the capital, Bishkek, taking the leading position as an FDI recipient, followed by the southern Osh region and the mineral-rich Issyk-Kul region. The Canadian mining company, Cameco Corporation, which is a key investor in the largest Kyrgyz gold mine, Kumtor, has been a major source of GDP and driver of GDP growth since 1992 in the country (ibid.). However, it is anticipated that gold production at Kumtor will end by 2008, which is likely to impact negatively the country's GDP.

Vanishing of 'obsolescing bargain'

The ability of transition host states to protect themselves against the inflow of 'malign' FDI and their aptitude in securing the inflow of 'benign' FDI can be significantly reduced not only by political instability, but also by shifts in bargaining power between host states and MNEs.

While Vernon and Moran, referring to 'obsolescing bargain', assumed that the position of MNEs *vis-à-vis* states can be significantly weakened once the foreign company has sunk investments which it cannot easily withdraw, Vernon acknowledges that the assumption that national leaders gained greater bargaining power as a result of growing competition between the firms was false. This has led him to suggest that 'overall, the role of multinational enterprises as a class has been growing, not declining' (Vernon 1971:194; Moran 1974:144). Similarly, Stopford came to the conclusion that 'governments, as a group, have indeed lost their bargaining power to MNEs as the possibilities for their collective action have diminished' (Stopford *et al.* 1991:215). They have suggested that 'intensifying competition among states seems to have been a more important force for weakening their bargaining power, than have changes in global competition among firms' (ibid.). They have further argued that while 'governments can maintain considerable power in their dealings with any one foreign firm' (ibid.), the competition for world market shares is likely to undermine their positions (ibid.).

Recent research has suggested that bargaining no longer defines the MNE–host relationship, and that bargaining irrelevance is reflected in a shift from a conflictive relationship to a more cooperative one (Haslam 2004:2). According to this research, these movements can be explained by changes in the strategy of both MNE and governments which conditionally define an end to the era of 'massive expropriation' (ibid.:3). Luo (2004) suggests:

> [I]n the beginning of the twenty-first century, the nature of the relationship between multinational corporations (MNC) and host governments could be best described as coopetition, that is a situation where cooperation and competition simultaneously function in increasingly interdependent MNC–government relations (MGR).

> In this context, cooperation reflects the elements of mutual accommodation and collaboration, where joint payoffs and goal accomplishment are sought by all parties based on their interdependent activities or resources. Competition reflects the elements of bargaining where private gains are sought at the expense of the other party's interests. (Luo 2004:1)

Extending this argument further, Ramamurti suggests that 'in the last decade relations between MNEs and host governments in developing countries changed from being predominantly adversarial and confrontational to being non-adversarial and cooperative' (Ramamurthi 2001:23). In addition, it has been argued that the regulative authority of international institutions and the growth in variability of international instruments regulating relations between MNEs and host states are reducing the relevance of 'obsolescing bargain'.

Haslam (2004:15) argues that, in the current neoliberal epoch, the scope for bargaining between states and MNEs has become very limited, as attempts to extract more surplus from foreign firms can result in the deterioration of the host country's reputation as a good investment climate. Most contemporary research suggests that 'obsolescing bargain' has become irrelevant primarily owing to the necessity of the states to create a comparatively advantageous investment climate under conditions of growing competition. In this context, it is usually assumed that national goals and the interests of the state coincide with those of state representatives or officials responsible for making decisions. In doing so, much of this research ignores the possibility of a divergence of national goals and the interests pursued by government officials. However, evidence exists that, in certain countries, state officials are directed not by national interests but rather by the private motives of personal gain. Therefore, the nature of their decision-making cannot effectively underpin their country's reputation but rather increases uncertainty.

'Blind bargaining' and FDI inflows in post-Soviet countries

While existing bargaining models provide a reasonable description of the nature of bargaining in MNE-host state bargaining relations, none of them captures the specific characteristics of bargaining in neo-patrimonial post-Soviet states. This chapter suggests that these characteristics can be summarized under the term 'blind bargaining'.

'Blind bargaining' describes the relationships between MNE and recipient states with regard to their ability to attract 'benign' FDI for the states where 'the specific model of interaction between state and society blocking social and economic development of this state' (Zon 2001:72) exists. So, 'blind bargaining' occurs where a 'patrimonial and predatory state' (ibid.:71) has developed, as in Ukraine, in other post-Soviet states and in states with analogous characteristics and behavioural patterns. It relates specifically to the 'deficiencies of these paralysing states' (ibid.) and helps explain inconsistencies in the bargaining behaviour of these states and their inability to attract quality FDI inflows.

'Blind bargaining' is rooted in the heterogeneity of bargaining interests of government actors in neo-patrimonial states and the incentive incompatibilities faced by officials. Neo-patrimonial states, in this context, can be defined as regimes possessing the following characteristics: high levels of personalization of power in the state, the capture of the state by ruling clans, a lack of the rule of law,[5] lack of distinction between the spheres of economics and politics, a disintegration of the state apparatus, the spread of corrupt practices in the state bureaucracy, the paralysing impact of state intervention in economic life (motivated by the personal interests of the representatives of state authorities), a lack of transparency and a lack of consistency in all spheres of political and economic life (Zon 2001:72–73).[6]

'Blind bargaining' reflects both the presence of a latent conflict between the national and personal interests of state representatives and the inability of the existing political system to sanction individual self-enrichment. As a consequence of this situation, the decisions of neo-patrimonial host states are often directed not towards serving national interests but towards supporting personal aims of the officials in power. This leads to bargains with these states being less stable and more unpredictable than those with states which are characterized by conventional patterns of economic instability such as, for instance, lack of currency convertibility.

One of the primary implications of 'blind bargaining' is the absence of any distinction between spheres of economy and politics. Moreover, there is a subordination of state politics to the personal economic interests of the ruling elite.

In many post-Soviet states, the rule of political–economic clans is omnipresent and it even shows 'dynastic' tendencies. In October

2003, for instance, for the first time, the rule of a post-Soviet state was passed from father to son as a result of Azerbaijan's 'democratic' presidential elections. In Kazakhstan, President Nursultan Nazarbayev's eldest daughter, the country's biggest media baron, is creating a new political party and is believed to be being groomed for the succession of her father. There is also an assumption that the head of the major business empire in Uzbekistan, the daughter of President Islam Karimov, would replace her father if he was forced to step down. Turkmenistan's President, Saprmurat Niyazov, is president for life. At least half of the former Soviet republics can be considered as being predominantly governed by authoritarian rule.

Relatives of presidents are often the biggest businessmen in their countries, possessing massive economic power. The daughter of Ukrainian President Leonid Kuchma is married to one of the country's oligarchs, a steel and media magnate. The son of the present president of Moldova and sons of the both previous presidents of this country are all-powerful business tycoons. Former Georgian President Eduard Shevardnadze's nephews and son-in-law are among the leaders of the country's biggest business clans (BBC News 2003:2).

The presidents of Ukraine and Belarus attempted to introduce constitutional changes to satisfy their wish to seek another presidential term. Lacking judiciary independence, the Ukrainian constitutional court ruled that Kuchma could stand for another term. In many post-Soviet republics the body of law that exists on paper is often arbitrarily interpreted and enforced so as to serve the personal goals of the elite. Moreover, laws are sometimes applied retroactively (WMRC 2004b: 2–3, 32; WMRC 2004i:1).

In Azerbaijan, for instance, President Aliyev is ultimately the sole guarantor of foreign investors' interests in a highly unstable socio-political situation. In late 2002, investors filed a US$300m. lawsuit against the president, his son and the former head of the country's privatization commission, over the aborted privatization of the state oil company, SOCAR (WMRC 2004b:33).

Regulatory uncertainty, weightiness of bureaucracy and corruption are primary characteristics of the post-Soviet investment environment. According to the Transparency International Corruption Perception Index, post-Soviet states ranked among the most corrupt in the world (see Table 4.3). Interestingly, all post-Soviet states were downgraded as a result of growing corruption during the years of transition.

In 2003, for instance, Ukraine, Moldova and Russia were ranked as 106th, 100th and 86th, respectively (out of 133 countries), while in 1999 they had occupied the 75th, 75th and 82nd places respectively (out of 99 countries). Among the Central European post-Soviet countries Belarus was the most successful in reducing corruption and ranked 53rd (out of 133) in 2003. Performing even worse, the Central Asian countries were ranked in the following sequence in 2003: Armenia 78th, Kazakhstan and Uzbekistan 100th, Kyrgyzstan 118th, Azerbaijan, Georgia and Tajikistan 124th, having being ranked between 80th and 90th in 1999 (Transparency International 2004:45).

Regarding post-Soviet countries, the World Market Research Centre concluded that 'flux in the regulatory environment and the overblown importance of bureaucracy have fuelled a high degree of corruption at different levels of the system' (WMRC 2004i:45). Further to this it was noted:

> [M]any officials, both at different levels of government and at the enterprise level, have vested interests in the status quo and see foreign firms as a threat and regional power groups use their influence in state agencies in order to secure as many economic benefits as possible. (Ibid.)

The report concludes that 'in the absence of transparent system, the ability to lobby and use a network of contacts has become a valued commodity' (ibid.).

Licensing requirements are vivid examples of flourishing corrupt practices and the maintenance of vested interests. In many sectors, such as transport and energy generation and distribution, the respective ministries are responsible for issuing licences to private investors while at the same time enjoying direct commercial interests in these sectors (WMRC 2004a:33). The presence of powerful interest groups and the importance of contacts create opportunities for the corruption and misuse of business relationships. More importantly, there is a possibility that bargaining outcomes may come up for re-examination if a contact is dismissed or replaced at their post (WMRC 2004c:27).

Government attempts to fight corruption have had, in many cases, more to do with politics and public image than with effective crusade

Table 4.3 Corruption perception indexes (CPIs) for post-Soviet states

Country	1997 Country rank/52	1997 CPI	1998 Country rank/85	1998 CPI	1999 Country rank/99	1999 CPI
1. Former USSR Countries						
1.1 Central and Eastern Europe						
1. Belarus	...	...	47	3.9	58	3.4
2. Moldova	...	...	...	...	75	2.6
3. Russia	49	2.27	76	2.4	82	2.4
4. Ukraine	...	...	69	2.8	75	2.6
1.2 Central Asia						
5. Armenia	...	...	...	...	80	2.5
6. Azerbaijan	...	...	...	...	96	1.7
7. Georgia	...	...	...	...	84	2.3
8. Kazakhstan	...	...	...	...	84	2.3
9. Kyrgyzstan	...	...	...	...	87	2.2
10. Tajikistan	...	...	...	...	...	...
11. Turkmenistan	...	...	...	...	...	...
12. Uzbekistan	...	...	...	...	94	1.8
1.3 Baltic countries/ EU accession countries						
13. Estonia	...	...	26	5.7	27	5.7
14. Latvia	...	...	71	2.7	58	3.4
15. Lithuania	...	...	...	...	50	3.8
2. Central and Eastern Europe						
2.1 EU Accession Countries						
16. Bulgaria	...	...	66	2.9	63	3.3
17. Czech Republic	27	5.2	37	4.8	39	4.6
18. Hungary	28	5.18	33	5.0	31	5.2
19. Poland	29	5.08	39	4.6	44	4.2
20. Romania	37	3.44	61	3.0	63	3.3
21. Slovakia	...	...	47	3.9	53	3.7
22. Slovenia	...	...	...	...	25	6.0
2.2 Other Countries						
23. Albania	...	...	...	...	84	2.3
24. Bosnia and Herzegovina	...	...	...	...	...	...
25. Croatia	...	...	...	...	74	2.7
26. Macedonia (TFYR)	...	...	...	...	63	3.3
27. Serbia and Montenegro	...	...	...	...	...	...

Source: Transparency International (2004).

Year							
2000		2001		2002		2003	
Country rank/90	CPI	Country rank/91	CPI	Country rank/102	CPI	Country rank/133	CPI
43	4.1	…	…	36	4.8	53	4.2
74	2.6	63	3.1	93	2.1	100	2.4
82	2.1	79	2.3	71	2.7	86	2.7
87	1.5	83	2.1	85	2.4	106	2.3
76	2.5	…	…	…	…	78	3.0
87	1.5	84	2.0	95	2.0	124	1.8
…	…	…	…	85	2.4	124	1.8
65	3.0	71	2.7	88	2.3	100	2.4
…	…	…	…	…	…	118	2.1
…	…	…	…	…	…	124	1.8
…	…	…	…	…	…	…	…
79	2.4	71	2.7	68	2.9	100	2.4
27	5.7	28	5.6	29	5.6	33	5.5
57	3.4	59	3.4	52	3.7	57	3.8
43	4.1	38	4.8	36	4.8	41	4.7
52	3.5	47	3.9	45	4.0	54	3.9
42	4.3	47	3.9	52	3.7	54	3.9
32	5.2	31	5.3	33	4.9	40	4.8
43	4.1	44	4.1	45	4.0	64	3.6
68	2.9	69	2.8	77	2.6	83	2.8
52	3.5	51	3.7	52	3.7	59	3.7
28	5.5	34	5.2	27	6.0	29	5.9
…	…	…	…	81	2.5	92	2.5
…	…	…	…	…	…	70	3.3
52	3.5	37	3.9	51	3.8	59	3.7
…	…	…	…	…	…	106	2.3
…	…	…	…	…	…	106	2.3

for transparency (WMRC 2004a:34). Currently, the lack of regulation and the over-reliance on personal links combine to create opportunities for organized crime, which itself has become major concern to foreign investors (ibid.).

'Blind bargaining', as a concept of bargaining, is characterized by multiple layers of risk-creating institutional and structural factors which jointly explain the lack of attractiveness of neo-patrimonial states to foreign investors. Additionally, the concept helps to explain why post-Soviet neo-patrimonial countries serve mostly as a target of riskier and lower-quality FDI, earlier referred as 'malign' FDI, which focuses on the exploitation of natural resources.

The following section investigates the role of country risks and certain economic indicators in determining FDI inflows into post-Soviet states.

Analysis of FDI inflows quality: 'malign' versus 'benign' FDI

The following analysis draws on the World Market Research Centre's data, which have been arranged in a panel format, listing variable scores for 27 post-Soviet and Eastern European countries for the five year period, 1998–2002.

Column 1 of Table 4.4 lists standardized slope coefficients (with *t*-value) and column 2 the coefficient of determination (R^2) for the bivariate regressions (unrestricted OLS) of 'FDI as per cent of GDP' with a series of independent variables. Ignoring problems of heteroscedasticity and autocorrelation, significant slope coefficients and substantial coefficients of variation can be detected for all of the country risk indicators, in particular, for 'overall country risk', 'political risk', 'economic risk', 'legal risk', 'tax risk' and 'operational risk',[7] all of which are negatively related to FDI (that is, the greater these risks, the lower is the relative FDI). Significant slope coefficients (at the 0.10 significance level) can be also detected for 'inflation', which regresses negatively with FDI, and 'exports per capita', which regresses positively with FDI. The variable 'trade balance' also produces a significant coefficient, which, interestingly, indicates a negative relationship between a balance of trade and FDI as well as 'debt per capita' does.

Next, the dependent variable 'FDI as per cent of GDP' is subjected to a multivariate OLS regression, which includes a number of

Table 4.4 Regression models for a sample of 27 post-Soviet and Eastern European countries, 1998–2002

Dependent variable: FDI as percentage of GDP.

	Unrestricted OLS		Restricted OLS	LSDV	GLSE
Models	**(1)**	**(2)**	**(3)**	**(4)**	**(5)**
Overall country risk	−1.924 (−3.807)	.098			
Political risk	−1.453 (−3.229)	.073			
Economic risk	−1.974 (−4.285)	.121	−2.979 (−4.808)	−0.934 (−0.402)	−2.833 (−2.942)
Legal risk	−1.907 (−3.785)	.097			
Tax risk	−1.915 (−3.405)	.080			
Operational risk	−0.989 (−2.150)	.034			
Security risk	−1.199 (−2.841)	.057			
Inflation	−0.025 (−2.435)	.043	−0.011 (−1.048)	0.007 (0.564)	0.002 (0.015)
Unemployment	0.035 (0.847)	.005	0.072 (1.795)	−0.059 (−0.341)	0.064 (0.970)
GDP per capita	0.0001 (0.706)	.004	−0.002 (−4.506)	−0.002 (−1.981)	−0.002 (−3.139)
Export per capita	0.0004 (1.469)	.016	0.003 (3.585)	0.004 (2.004)	0.003 (2.622)
Trade balance	−0.0001 (−1.566)	.018	−0.000 (−1.045)	−0.000 (−0.507)	−0.000 (−0.893)
Debt per capita	−0.003 (−0.283)	.001	−0.014 (−1.252)	−0.018 (−0.605)	−0.013 (−0.815)
			0.258	0.586	0.213

t-values are listed in parentheses.

Unadjusted and adjusted coefficients of determination (R^2) are listed next to the slope parameter or at the bottom of the column respectively.

Source: Data from World Market Research Centre.

independent variables that were selected on the basis of their conceptual relevancy and a desire to avoid multicollinearity in the model. Using such a constant-coefficients (or pulled-regression) model with panel data has a number of statistical drawbacks. However, following Stimson (1985), this model can be used as a computational basis for more efficient models such as the general least-squares errors (GLSE) model. Column 3 of Table 4.4 again lists standardized coefficients (with *t*-values) and the overall coefficient of determination (R^2) for this OLS model. This model yields significant negative slopes for the variables 'economic risk' and 'GDP per capita'. Significant positive coefficients can be detected (albeit only at the 0.10 level of significance) for 'export per capita' and for 'unemployment' (see Table 4.4, column 3). Given the limited significance of these variables, the model yields a relatively large coefficient of determination with 25.8 per cent. This is likely to be a reflection of a violation of statistical assumptions, which arise from the use of panel data.

Next, the same data are subjected to a fixed-effects (or least-squares-dummy-variable (LSDV)) model. In terms of significance of coefficients, this LSDV estimation produces much weaker results than the previous OLS models. Thus, significant coefficients can be detected only for 'GDP per capita', which again yields a negative coefficient, and 'export per capita', which yields a positive coefficient (see Table 4.4, column 4). Despite this, the LSDV model produces a relatively high coefficient of determination, with 58.6 per cent of total variation being explained by the model.

Following Stimson (1985), information from the OLS and LSDV models can be used to estimate an error parameter, which is then used to calculate the much more reliable GLSE model.[8] Overall, the results of the GLSE model mirror closely the results of the LSDV model. Thus, a significant negative relationship can be detected for 'economic risk' and 'GDP per capita', while 'export per capita' yields a positive coefficient (see Table 4.4, column 5). Explaining 21.3 per cent of the variation, the coefficient of determination indicates that the model fits every country sample reasonably well, with the possibility of significant heterogeneity existing between different groups of countries.

The analysis based on the GLSE model is then repeated for different subgroups of countries (see Table 4.5). The first subgroup includes 10 EU accession countries only (Bulgaria, Czech Republic, Estonia, Hungary, Latvia, Lithuania, Poland, Romania, Slovakia, Slovenia). Again, the model yields significant negative coefficients for 'economic risk' and 'GDP per capita' and a significant positive coefficient for 'export per capita' (see Table 4.5, column 1). This indicates that, while economic risk does negatively influence investment inflows, foreign investors are not keen to target richer and presumably politically more assertive accession states. Analysis of ex-Soviet republics (excluding the Baltic states) produces a slightly different pattern of relations. Here only the 'economic risk' variable gives a significant and, again, negative slope (see Table 4.5, column 2). Another potentially significant relationship exists with 'trade balance', which is also negatively correlated with FDI.

Table 4.5 General least-squares errors regressions for different subgroups of post-Soviet countries, 1998–2002

Dependent variable: FDI as percentage of GDP.

Subgroups	EU accession countries[a] (1)	Post-Soviet countries (excluding Baltics)[b] (2)	Post-Soviet European countries[c] (3)	Post-Soviet Central Asian countries[d] (4)
Economic risk	−2.185	−7.411	−4.324	−8.233
	(−2.069)	(−2.514)	(−1.021)	(−1.951)
Inflation	−0.007	0.006	0.007	0.008
	(−0.202)	(0.395)	(0.969)	(0.094)
Unemployment	0.115	−0.012	−0.231	−0.002
	(1.408)	(−0.061)	(−1.392)	(−0.006)
GDP per capita	−0.002	−0.000	0.000	−0.003
	(−3.144)	(−0.037)	(0.349)	(−0.698)
Export per capita	0.003	−0.000	0.003	0.028
	(3.076)	(−0.047)	(0.454)	(1.904)
Trade balance	−0.000	−0.000	−0.000	−0.006
	(−0.466)	(−1.043)	(−1.068)	(−2.378)
Debt per capita	−0.012	−0.007	0.078	−0.014
	(−0.472)	(−0.249)	(1.777)	(−0.307)
	R^2 = 0.194	R^2 = 0.128	R^2 = 0.462	R^2 = 0.259

[a] Bulgaria, Czech Republic, Estonia, Hungary, Latvia, Lithuania, Poland, Romania, Slovakia, Slovenia.

[b] Armenia, Azerbaijan, Belarus, Georgia, Kazakhstan, Kyrgyzstan, Moldova, Russia, Tajikistan, Turkmenistan, Ukraine, Uzbekistan.

[c] Belarus, Moldova, Russia, Ukraine.

[d] Armenia, Azerbaijan, Georgia, Kazakhstan, Kyrgyzstan, Tajikistan, Turkmenistan, Uzbekistan.

t-values are listed in parenthesis.

Unadjusted and adjusted coefficients of determination (R^2) are listed next to the slope parameter or at the bottom of the column respectively.

Source: Data from World Market Research Centre.

For the European ex-Soviet republics (excluding the Baltic states), namely Belarus, Moldova, Russia and Ukraine, the same GLSE model yields an impressive coefficient of determination of 46.2 per cent. This, however, is not reflected in terms of significant coefficients. Thus, potentially significant coefficients can be detected only for 'debt per capita', which yields a positive slope, and 'unemployment', which yields a negative one. The former coefficient is indicative of the assumption on the predominance of 'malign' FDI inflows to these countries, which is debt-increasing but not necessarily employment-reducing (see Table 4.5, column 3).

Lastly, the GLSE model is applied to the subgroup of ex-Soviet Central Asian republics. It produces significant negative coefficients for 'economic risk' and 'trade balance' and a significant positive coefficient for 'export per capita' (see Table 4.5, column 4).

Taken together, these subgroup analyses suggest that the prospect of attracting 'malign' FDI is most profound in those post-Soviet European countries which are not accessing to the EU (Belarus, Moldova, Russia and Ukraine). Meanwhile, among accession countries in particular, there is evidence that foreign investors are becoming more reluctant to invest into those countries which have achieved certain levels of wealth and, presumably, institutional capacity.

Conclusion

This chapter argues that the failure of post-Soviet states to attract the required amounts of quality FDI can be, first of all, explained by the presence of 'blind bargaining'. 'Blind bargaining' originates from the specific state and society relationship which can be formed in neo-patrimonial host states where economic decisions are often directed not towards serving national interests, but rather towards supporting the personal aims of the officials in power. 'Blind bargaining', which ultimately undermines the relationships between MNEs and such neo-patrimonial host states, reflects both the presence of the latent conflict between the national and personal interests of the state representatives and the inability of the existing political system to sanction individual self-enrichment.

It can be argued that the subordination of state politics to the personal economic interests of a ruling elite, as a main characteristic underpinning the existence of 'blind bargaining', explains the inability of many post-Soviet states to attract the required amounts of quality FDI. It also explains the attractiveness of these states to riskier investors and consequently the inflows of mostly 'malign' FDI into these countries.

Our comparative analysis of the impact of these countries' risks and the economic indicators on the quality of interactions between FDI and host states, conducted for 27 post-Soviet and CEE countries, supports the main argument of this chapter, in that it documents the differential relationships between the FDI inflows and the other variables for different groups of countries. These include all post-Soviet states except the Baltic states, the Central European accession and non-accession countries, the Central European post-Soviet states and the Central Asian states.

The most stable relationship that can be observed for all groupings is the strong correlation between FDI and the levels of economic risks. The significance and strength of this attests to the significance of the 'blind bargaining' context, since one of the main criteria upon which WMRC bases its rating of this type of risk is policy consistency and the forward planning of the economy. The latter is, first of all, dependent on the quality and independence of a state's economic and political system, a lack of which reflects a latent conflict between genuine economic goals and the private interests of the ruling elite, which in turn creates high levels of uncertainty and instability with regard to policies.

Interesting also are, primarily the negative (though not very significant) relationship between FDI and 'GDP per capita' and, secondarily, the weak negative relationship between FDI and 'trade balance'. The former supports the assumption, made on the basis of the previous research, that FDI flows to European EU accession countries in particular decrease with an increase in welfare levels in these countries.

Further to this, it can be observed that a negative relation between FDI and 'trade balance', which is much stronger for the Central Asian countries, coexists with a positive relationship between FDI and 'export per capita' for this region. This appears to indicate that resource-centred FDI is likely to increase per capita export. However, these gains are wiped out by excessive public and private spending, which negatively affects the country's overall trade balance.

The relationships between FDI and some other economic indicators provide further evidence for this chapter's argument. Thus, EU accession countries are the only group for which FDI is negatively correlated with inflation. By contrast, in all post-Soviet states, FDI inflows are not associated with the reduction of the rates of inflation. Moreover, in case of the post-Soviet European states FDI shows a strong positive relationship with 'debt per capita', while for all other groups this relationship is weakly negative. This indicates that this region attracts riskier and lower-quality debt-increasing investment.

The opposite situation can be observed for 'unemployment'. Here, EU accession countries are the only group for which unemployment reveals a strong enough (in comparison with all other cases) positive relationship with FDI *vis-à-vis* post-Soviet countries where FDI is negatively related with unemployment. This finding, though contradictory to the original argument on lower FDI quality in neo-patrimonial post-Soviet states, indicates that EU accession countries are now attracting FDI which is not contributing to the increase of employment in the region. The inference can be made that, after reaching a certain level of development by transition countries, FDI changes its quality from being unemployment-reducing to not contributing to the increase in employment. The negative relationship between unemployment and FDI in case of post-Soviet European countries, in turn, can be explained by the high levels of underreporting figures on unemployment in these states.

In general, it can be concluded that there is quantitative evidence for lower-quality FDI inflows into neo-patrimonial post-Soviet states. However, further country- and industry-specific analyses are required to ascertain variations in the relationship between country (and industry) characteristics and the nature of FDI inflows.

Acknowledgements

Nataliya Ass would like to thank Professor John Ravenhill and Professor Russel Keat, of the University of Edinburgh for their comments and advice on her previous work on this topic.

Notes

1. 'Benign' FDI is the term applied to FDI capable of bringing about the following possible positive effects for a developing and transition host country: transfer of capital; transfer of know-how and management; increased efficiency and expansion of output; higher economic growth;

balance of payments benefits; increased competition and lower prices; increased entrepreneurial spirit; help in training and education; increased employment; help in infrastructure; improved living conditions in developing countries; identification, allocation, management and effective use of world material and human and financial resources; greater international unity and interdependency; securing a more equal distribution of income and wealth.

2. 'Malign' FDI is the term applied to FDI imposing some of the following costs on a recipient economy and bearing the following possible negative characteristics: hampering of balance of payments; ousting domestic producers out of business; contributing to the decrease of domestic saving and investments; production of import-substitution outputs instead of export-oriented products; export of profits and interest; use of technology too advanced for a country and too capital-intensive; limited training and education; input of foreign management to the neglect of local managers; curbing of local enterprises; enforcement of consumption functions (luxury items); uneven distribution of income; negative effect on employment; transfer of know-how restricted and beneficial spillovers and externalities prevented; subordination of companies and countries to multinational enterprises; national sovereignty threatened; endogenous socio-economic development of the country hampered; recession resulting from the inability of national industries to compete; loss of national pride and nationalist spirit.
3. Some of the components of the inward FDI potential index are: country's inward FDI stock and exports of natural resources and service as a share of the world's total flows; country risk; total exports and research and development expenditures as a percentage of GDP; GDP and commercial energy use per capita; real GDP growth; total exports and several other indicators considered as capable of affecting an economy's attractiveness to foreign investors.
4. This indirectly confirms a hypothesis that FDI investors prefer weaker countries and reduce investments once these states become politically stable and more assertive. (This indirectly confirms a hypothesis that the share of FDI inflows in the total capital flows to the country tends to decrease with the strengthening of the state.)
5. The wish of rulers always prevails over the law.
6. These are not caused primarily by a lack of competence but are often created deliberately.
7. WMRC estimates its risk indicators on the basis of the following criteria:
   - Political risk (*PR*): institutional performance, represetativeness, internal political consensus, external political consensus;
   - Economic risk (*ER*): degree of market orientation, policy consistency and forward planning, diversity and resilience of the economy, macroeconomic fundamentals;
   - Legal risk (*LR*): legislation, transparency, independence, experience;
   - Tax risk (*TR*): coherence, fairness, level, effectiveness;

- Operational risk (*OR*): attitudes to foreign investment, infrastructural quality, labour, bureaucracy and corruption;
- Security risk (*SR*): civil unrest, crime, terrorism, external security threat.

Overall country risk (*OCR*):

$$OCR = \sqrt{(0.25\,PR^2 + 0.25\,ER^2 + 0.15\,LR^2 + 0.15\,TR^2 + 0.10\,OR^2 + 0.10\,SR^2)}$$

Risks are rated on the scale from 1 to 5 points, where 1 is insignificant risk and 5 is extreme risk.

8. Stimson (1985) notes that his error-components model performs well for 'short (in time) and fat (in space) design' which makes ideally suited to this analysis.

References

BBC News (2003) 'Dynasties of the Ex-USSR', available at http://www.bbc.com, accessed 16 September 2003.

Cornia, G. A. and Popov, V. (2001) *Transition and Institutions: The Experience of Gradual and Late Reformers*. Oxford: Oxford University Press, p. 270.

Elo, K.Z. (2003) 'Quality of Foreign Direct Investments under Country Risk with Incomplete Markets', Preliminary PhD Thesis, 3. Melbourne Institute of Applied Economic and Social Research, The University of Melbourne.

Gudkevych, S.A. (2001) 'Usloviya Privlecheniya Inostrannix Investitsii v Economiku Ukrainy' (Conditions for Attracting Foreign Investment into the Ukrainian Economy), *Finance and Credit*, 5–6, 55–9.

Haslam, P. A. (2004) 'The Bargaining Gap: Explaining the Stability of Domestic Foreign Investment Regimes and the Limitations on State-MNE Bargaining in a Globalized Economy', paper presented at the 8th International Business Conference, Guadalajara, Mexico.

Hausmann, R. and Fernandez-Arias, E. (2000) 'Foreign Direct Investment: Good Cholesterol?', paper presented at the seminar 'The New Wave of Capital inflows: Sea Change or Just Another Tide?', Annual Meeting of the Board of Governors, Inter-American Development Bank and Inter-American Investment Corporation, New Orleans, 46.

Lazebnyk, L. (1997) 'Investytsiinyi Klimat ta Ekonomichna Motyvatsiya Inozemnogo Investuvannya v Ukraini' (Investment Climate and Economic Motivation of Foreign Direct Investment in Ukraine), *Finance of Ukraine*, 4, 82–8.

Luo, Y. (2004) 'A Coopetition Perspective of MNC-Host Government Relations', paper presented at the European Applied Business Research Conference, Venice, Italy.

Maxmudov, A. (1998) 'Invstitsionnaya Politika Vixoda iz Depressii' (Investment Policy: The Way Out of Depression), *Economy of Ukraine*, 5, 39–40.

Moran, T. (1998) *FDI and Development: The New Policy Agenda for Developing Countries and Economics in Transition*. Washington, DC: Institute for International Economics, pp. 19–20.

Ramamurti, R. (2001) 'The "Obsolescing Bargaining Model"? MNC-Host Developing Countries Relations Revisited', *Journal of International Business Studies*, 32 (1), 23–38.

State Statistics Committee of Ukraine (1996–2002) *Statystychnyi Shorichnyk Ukrainy: 1995–2001* (Statistical Yearbook of Ukraine for 1995–2001). Kiev: Texnika.

Stopford, J., Strange S. and Hensley, J. (1991) *Rival States, Rival Firms: Competition for World Market Shares*. Cambridge University Press.

Transparency International (2004) 'Corruption Perception Index', available at http://www.transparency.org, accessed 05 May 2004.

UNCTAD (2001) *World Investment Report – 2001: Promoting Linkages*, New York: United Nations, p. 1.

UNCTAD (2003) *World Investment Report – 2003: FDI Policies for Development: National and International Perspective*. New York: United Nations, pp. xiii, 1.

Vernon, R. (1971) *Sovereignty at Bay: The Multinational Spread of US Enterprises*. London: Longman, p. 14.

WMRC (2004a) 'WMRC Country Report: Azerbaijan (Country Analysis and Forecast)', available at http://www.worldmarketanalysis.com, accessed 27 April 2004.

WMRC (2004b) 'WMRC Country Report: Belarus (Country Analysis and Forecast)', available at http://www.worldmarketanalysis.com, accessed 27 April 2004.

WMRC (2004c), 'WMRC Country Report: Georgia (Country Analysis and Forecast)', available at http://www.worldmarketanalysis.com, accessed 27 April 2004.

WMRC (2004d) 'WMRC Country Report: Kazakhstan (Country Analysis and Forecast)', available at http://www.worldmarketanalysis.com, accessed 27 April 2004.

WMRC (2004e) 'WMRC Country Report: Kyrgyzstan (Country Analysis and Forecast)', available at http://www.worldmarketanalysis.com, accessed 27 April 2004).

WMRC (2004f) 'WMRC Country Report: Moldova (Country Analysis and Forecast)', available at http://www.worldmarketanalysis.com, accessed 27 April 2004.

WMRC, (2004g) 'WMRC Country Report: Russia (Country Analysis and Forecast)', available at http://www.worldmarketanalysis.com, accessed 27 April 2004.

WMRC (2004h) 'WMRC Country Report: Turkmenistan (Country Analysis and Forecast)', available at http://www.worldmarketanalysis.com, accessed 27 April 2004.

WMRC (2004i) 'WMRC Country Report: Ukraine (Country Analysis and Forecast)', available at http://www.worldmarketanalysis.com, accessed 27 April 2004.

Yacheistova, N. (2001) 'Russian Experience Regarding the Competition Policy on FDI Flows', *paper presented to the OECD Global Forum on International Investment*, Mexicocity, Mexico, pp. 11–12.

Zaxarin, S. (2000) 'Strategiya Pidvyshennya Investytsiinoi Pryvablyvosti Ekonomiky Ukrainy dlya Inozemnogo Kapitalu' (A Strategy for Increasing the Attractiveness of the Ukrainian Economy to Foreign Capital), *Finance of Ukraine*, 12, 88–89.
Zon, H. V. (2001) 'Neo-Patrimonialism as an Impediment to Economic Development: The Case of Ukraine', *Journal of Communist Studies and Transition Economies*, 17(3), 71–95.

Bibliography

Bachrach, P. and M.S. Baratz (1970) *Power and Poverty: Theory and Practice*. New York: Oxford University Press, p. 220.
Bacharach, R. and E.J. Lawler (1981) *Bargaining: Power, Tactics, and Outcomes*. San Francisco: Jossy-Bass, p. 234.
Baun, D. (1999) 'Mozhlyvosti ta Ryzyky dlya Inozemnyx Investytsii v Ukrainskyi Gazovyi Sector' (Opportunities and risks for Foreign Investment in the Ukrainian Gas Sector), *Economist*, 6, 68–72. Kyiv, Ukraine.
Benderskii, E. (1998) 'Rol Investitsii I Innovatsii v Restructurizatsii Ekonomiky' (The Role of Investments and Innovations in the Economy Restructuring), *Economy of Ukraine*, 9, 37–48. Kyiv, Ukraine.
Danko, M. (1999), 'Innovatiinyi Potentsial u Promyslovosty Ukrainy' (Novelty Potential of Ukrainian Industry), *Economist*, 10, 29–32. Kyiv, Ukraine.
Dyker, D. (1999) *Foreign Direct Investment and Technology Transfer in the Former Soviet Union*. Cheltenham: Elgar, p. 205.
Filipenko, A. (1997) 'Osoblyvosti Rozvytku Inozemnogo Investuvannya v Economiku Ukrainy', (Distinctive Features of Foreign Investment in Ukrainian Economy), *Finance of Ukraine*, 2, 81–3.
Hay, C. (1997) 'Divided by a Common Language: Political Theory and Concept of Power', *Politics*, 1(17), 45–52.
IMF (2003) *Ukraine: Selected Issues*, IMF Country Reports, no. 03/173, 69.
Kovalishin, P. and A. Starostin (1999) 'Problemy Inozemnogo Investuvannya' (Problems of Foreign Investment), *Finance of Ukraine*, 11, 78–85.
Kulchytskyi, M. (1998) 'Investytsiine Zabezpechennya Rozvvytku Vyrobnychoi sfery' (Investment Provision of Industry Development), *Finance of Ukraine*, 5, 11–13.
Kuxlenko, O., M. Denysenko and S. Revutskyi (1998) *Investytsii v Ukraini: Suchasnyi Stan, Problemy, Perspektyvy Rozvytku* (Investments in Ukraine: Contemporary Situation, Problems, and Perspectives for Development), Kyiv: Vakler, pp. 31–33.
Lehmann, A. (2002) 'The Distribution of Fixed Capital in the Multinational Firm', *IMF Staff Papers*, 49(1), 136–153.
Lukes, S. (1980) *Power: A Radical View*, London: Macmillan, p. 64.
Mar'enko, A., G. Printch, N. Patika and K. Prib (1999) 'Problema Zaluchennya Inozemnyx Investytsii v Ekonomiku Ukrainy' (Problem of Attraction of Foreign Investment into Ukrainian Economy), *Economy of Ukraine*, 7, 30–8.

Meyer, K.E. and Pind, C. (1999) 'The Slow Growth of Foreign Direct Investment in the Soviet Union Successor States', *Economics of Transition*, 7(1), 201–14.
Moran, T. (1998) *FDI and Development: The New Policy Agenda for Developing Countries and Economics in Transition*. Washington, DC: Institute for International Economics, pp. 19–21.
PRS Group Inc. (2001) 'International Country Risk Guide', available at http://www.prsgroup.com, 21(9), accessed 25 January 2002.
PRS Group Inc. (2001) 'International Country Risk Guide', available at http://www.prsgroup.com, 24(3), accessed 21 February 2004.
Rubtsova, M. (1999) *Natsionalni Osoblyvosti Formuvannya Investytsiinogo Klimatu dlya Zaluchennya Inozemnogo Kapitalu v Ukrainu* (National Peculiarities of Investment Climate Creation for Attraction of Foreign Capital in Ukraine). Kiev: NANU, p. 2.
Stimson, J. (1985) 'Regression in Space and Time: A Statistical Essay', *American Journal of Political Science*, 29, 4, 914–47.
Tkach, T. (1999), 'Rol Inozemnyx Investytsii v Ekonomitsi Ukrainy' (The Role of Foreign Investments in the Ukrainian Economy), *Finance of Ukraine*, 9, 27–35.
WMRC (2004j) 'WMRC Country Report: Armenia (Country Analysis and Forecast)', available at http://www.worldmarketanalysis.com, accessed 27 April 2004, 25.
WMRC (2004k) 'WMRC Country Report: Uzbekistan (Country Analysis and Forecast)', available at http://www.worldmarketanalysis.com, accessed 27 April 2004, 34.
Woolfson, C. and Beck, M. (2004) 'The End of Labour Quiescence? Undustrial Unrest in Contemporary Lithuania', *International Journal of Comparative Labour Law and Industrial Relations*, 20(1), 227–52.

5

Foreign Exchange Risk Management in Emerging Markets: The Case of Malaysia

Ahmad Shukri Yazid and Mohd Shaladdin Muda

Introduction

The Asian financial crisis of 1997 shook many multinationals in the Asian markets with problems caused by wild fluctuations in the exchange rates of many countries in the region. Many of the multinationals were exposed themselves to the foreign exchange risk, so that the subject became one of hot debate among the top managements.

The lack of foreign exchange risk management is one of the factors contributing to major financial losses among multinationals in Asia. According to Mohd Azwar Mahmud, general manager of the Malaysian Monetary Exchange Bhd, very few Malaysian multinationals actively managed currency risk (*New Straits Times*, 30 May 1998). Therefore, not surprisingly, many authors such as Berkman and Bradbury (1996) and Smithson *et al.* (1995) and Froot *et al.* (1994) suggested that foreign exchange risk management can help multinationals to eliminate or reduce currency risk.

There are several ways to define foreign exchange risk management. For example, Ankrom (1974) saw it as the management of transaction, translation and economic exposures. Chiu and Foerster (1997) suggested that foreign exchange risk management should include the identification and determination of risk, the choice and implementation of the most appropriate financial instruments, and finally the evaluation of the risk management programme. However, this chapter defines foreign exchange risk management as a process aimed at avoiding or minimizing transaction, translation and economic exposures using financial tools such as forwards, futures, options and swaps.

The aim of this chapter is to examine the foreign exchange risk management practices among the Malaysian multinationals. In particular, it investigates the influence of managers' ethnic groups towards the management of currency risk. It also provides an insight into how Malaysian multinationals manage their currency exposures.

The structure of this chapter is as follows. In the next section, the literature reviews on financial risk management are described in detail. At the same time, the specific characteristics of the Malaysian managers are described so as to explain the need for a study on Malaysian foreign exchange risk management. In the third section, the process of collecting survey questionnaires is discussed. The result of the survey questionnaires is then presented in the fourth section, while conclusions are drawn in the fifth section.

Literature reviews

Much of the recent literature in financial risk management focuses on the management of foreign exchange risk (for example, Geczy 1997; Makar and Huffman 1997; Wallace 1998;). In addition, it is argued that foreign exchange risk management can be used to mitigate currency risk (Froot *et al.* 1994; Smithson *et al.* 1995; Berkman and Bradbury 1996).

Several studies have been undertaken in developed countries such as the USA, UK and Australia. A recent study of the US non-financial firms by Bodnar *et al.* (1996) gave a detailed scenario of the management of financial risk. One important finding of this study is that 83 per cent of large firms used financial instruments, compared with 45 per cent and 12 per cent of medium and small firms. The result is predictable since large firms have more resources than medium and small ones.

A survey by Belk and Glaum *et al.* (1990) on 17 major UK companies found that the majority (94 per cent) centralized foreign exchange risk management activities at the parent company. Dealing with attitudes towards risk-taking behaviour Belk and Glaum (1990) found that most of UK companies were totally risk-averse, while a few aimed to gain from foreign exchange movements and hedged partially.

In the Malaysian context, very few studies are known on the management of foreign exchange risk. A limited number of derivatives can be found on the Malaysian market. Forward contracts are offered by local banks in the country. For this reason, it appears that prior to 1997 there are very few multinationals involved in foreign exchange risk management activities.

Studies of risk-taking behaviour are important in determining managers' perceptions of risk. Accordingly, MacCrimmon and Wehrung (1990) surveyed 500 top-level business executives to ascertain the validity of common stereotypes regarding risk-taking and risk-avoidance behaviours. Interestingly, they found that successful managers are the biggest risk-takers while mature managers tended to be risk-averse. Such behaviour by the older managers was probably owing to their secure positions within their companies.

Douglas and Wildavsky (1982) argued that managers' culture might influence their risk-taking behaviour. In the Malaysian context, managers working in various companies may come from different ethnic groups. The majority of these managers are either Malays or Chinese. Owing to their different cultures, it is to be expected that their behaviours towards risk will differ. This is supported by Abdullah's (1996) extensive study of the attitudes of managers from different ethnic groups. She found that Malay managers are risk-averse while Chinese managers are more willing to take risk. Since Malay managers are risk-averse, they are expected to be more involved in the foreign exchange risk management activities than are the Chinese. In addition, as suggested by Gomez (1999), the Chinese managers have more experience in international businesses. Therefore, it can be argued that this experience may lead them to be less involved in risk management.

Methodology

Many studies of foreign exchange risk management have employed questionnaire surveys (for example, Malindretos and Tsanacas 1995; Joseph and Hawins 1997; Bodnar *et al.* 1998). Saunders *et al.* (1997) claimed that there are three main advantages in questionnaires. First, they are highly economical since a large amount of data can be collected from a big population. Second, they can be standardized, making for easy comparisons. Finally, they are easily understood by most people.

For the purpose of this study only multinationals listed on the Bursa Malaysia (previously the Kuala Lumpur Stock Exchange) are selected. These companies are heavily involved in international transactions. Therefore they are likely to be exposed to currency risk. A total of 90 multinationals were identified out of a population of 113. In order to increase response rate, the corporate treasurers or financial directors of these multinationals, identified by name, had questionnaires sent directly to them. A second reminder was sent after three weeks if there was no response. Out of the 90 multinationals, 54 responded, a 61 per cent response rate.

The high response rate is probably owing to the participants' interest in the study. The subject is highly topical following the heavy losses suffered by the multinationals concerned during the crisis period. This conclusion is supported by Vaus (1993), who argued that a combination of factors such as the nature of the topic and the sample, the length of the questionnaire and other factors like the timing of the survey influenced the response rate.

The majority (80 per cent) of those who did not respond did so owing to work pressure, especially that from preparing year-end reports (Table 5.1). A total of 14.3 per cent did not want to participant in the survey while another 5.7 per cent did not respond owing to company policy.

Table 5.1 Companies' reasons for not responding to the foreign exchange risk management questionnaire

Reason	**% (number)**
Busy/work pressure	80 (28)
Did not want to participate	14.3 (5)
Company policy	5.7 (2)
Total	100 (35)

Results and analyses

Perceptions of major and financial risks

The study examines how managers perceive major risks related to their businesses. Major risks are business, financial, and political risks. Business risks involve uncertainties about the company's overall activities owing to events in the market which are outside its control and might result to financial losses. Financial risks involve interest rates, foreign exchange risks and commodity price risks. Political risks involve uncertainties arising from policies made by national governments and governments abroad.

As shown in Table 5.2, among managers who managed financial risks, about 55 per cent gave the highest priority to business risks in the period before the crisis as compared to about 18 per cent and 3 per cent for financial risks and political risks. This result may suggest ignorance on the part of many managers about financial risks during this period. During the financial crisis, their perceptions of risks changed dramatically. The percentage that attributed the highest priority to financial risks and political risks increased to about 82 per cent and 18 per cent, respectively. The percentage for business risks decreased slightly to about 52 per cent. Meanwhile, in the current period, the percentages for business risks, financial risks and political risks are about 70 per cent, 64 per cent and 27 per cent, respectively.

For managers who did not manage financial risks, 50 per cent gave business risks the highest priority in the period before the crisis as compared with only about 17 per cent who put financial risks first (Table 5.3). During the crisis period, about 67 per cent gave the highest priority to financial risks as compared with only 44 per cent for business risks. However, for the current period, 63 per cent put

Table 5.2 Managers' perceptions of major risks for multinationals with foreign exchange risk management

Type of major risk	Periods		
	Before crisis	**During crisis**	**Current period**
Business risk	55	52	70
Financial risk	18	82	64
Political risk	3	18	27

Table 5.3 Managers' perceptions of major risks for multinationals without foreign exchange risk management

Type of major risks	Periods		
	Before crisis	During crisis	Current period
Business risk	50	44	63
Financial risk	17	67	21
Political risk	07	0	57

business risks first while the percentage giving top place to financial risks decreased to 21 per cent.

The survey also indicated that about 30 per cent of managers in multinationals who practise financial risk management attributed the highest priority to foreign exchange risk in the period before the crisis (Table 5.4). As expected, this percentage increased to about 88 per cent during the crisis and declined again to 49 per cent for the current period. Thus, only after the crisis did managers begin to pay significant attention to foreign exchange risk. On the other hand, the percentages for managers in multinationals without financial risk management who perceived foreign exchange risk as the most important were 28 per cent (before) 28 per cent (during) and 31 per cent (after), for the three periods, respectively.

As expected, managers in multinationals who managed financial risks gave more priority to financial risks as compared with managers in multinationals who were not involved in financial risk management. Despite that, financial risks were given less priority in the period before crisis. Thus, managers in these multinationals gave less priority to interest rates, foreign exchange and commodity price risks. This could be due to the stability of the Malaysian dollar and the economic boom. However, these managers gave a higher priority to financial risks during the crisis when the movement of the Malaysian currency was unpredictable. At the same time, perhaps because many of them were highly leveraged, they attributed a greater significant to interest rate risk. On the whole, among the three financial risks, foreign exchange risk was given the highest priority, especially during the crisis.

In the current period, after the government had imposed the capital and currency controls, the percentage of managers who gave higher

Table 5.4 Managers' perceptions of financial risks for multinationals with foreign exchange risk management

Type of financial risk	Periods		
	Before crisis	During crisis	Current period
Interest rate	24	55	46
Foreign exchange	30	88	49
Commodity price	15	12	27

priority to financial risks declined again. Simultaneously, the percentage of managers giving top priority to interest rate, foreign exchange and commodity price risks also declined. Even though foreign exchange risk is now less significant owing to the pegging of the Malaysian dollar against the US dollar, multinationals are still exposed to foreign exchange risk.

On the whole, the political risks were given the least priority for these three periods under consideration. This may be due to relative stability of many countries in the region. However, during the crisis period, the number of multinationals who gave a greater priority to political risks increased slightly. This could have been due to increased political instability both at home and abroad.

Possible reasons for the limited attention given to political risk by many multinationals include the huge devaluation of the Malaysian dollar and uncertainties in the interest rates during the crisis, which may have distracted managers from political problems.

Those managers of multinationals who did not practice risk management gave less priority to financial risks as compared with those multinational managers who did not practice foreign exchange risk management. Instead, business risks were the highest priority before the crisis. Later on, they gave the highest priority to interest rate risks, probably because many of them were highly leveraged. On the other hand, foreign exchange risk management was given less priority owing to the relatively small foreign currency exposures.

Manager traits

The manager characteristics observed in this study include the effects of age, experience and ethnic group on the practices of foreign exchange risk management.

As shown in Table 5.5, different age groups of managers differed significantly in their perceptions of major risks in the period before crisis. In particular, about 56 per cent of the older managers gave the highest priority to business risks compared with 11 per cent of the younger managers. This could be owing to a broadening definition of business risk, which includes all uncertainties in relation to the operations of multinationals. Older managers attributed the highest priority to financial risks during the crisis and in the current period. It seems that younger managers managed less short-term transaction exposures than did older managers. Overall, the younger managers were more proactive and more willing to take risks, while the older ones were risk-averse and more conservative. As suggested by MacCrimmon and Wehrung (1990), this could be because older managers have less opportunity to correct their mistakes. Moreover, younger managers may have much to gain from taking risks because they are at early stage of their career, when success offers opportunities for career development.

As suggested earlier, the experiences of managers may have affected their risk perceptions. It was found that experienced managers

Table 5.5 Managers' traits and risk perception – Kruskal–Wallis test

	Chi-square value
Age	*Before crisis* Business risks – 6.179* Financial risks – 10.944*** Political risks – 7.056*
Experience	*Before crisis* Commodity price risk – 6.917* *During crisis* Interest rate risk – 7.668** *Current period* Interest rate risk – 7.770**
Ethnic groups	*Before crisis* Financial risks – 6.669*** *Current period* Financial risks – 2.610**

* significant at 20%.
** significant at 10%.
*** significant at 5%.

differed significantly from others in their perception of financial risk during the current period (Table 5.5). About 50 per cent of the experienced managers gave greater priority to financial risks compared with those with less experience (27 per cent). However, experience did not influence their perception of risk before and during the crisis. Presumably, managers tended to ignore financial risks in the period before the crisis. During the crisis, a majority of managers irrespective of experience gave greater priority to financial risks. This could have been due to the significant financial losses suffered by many multinationals during the crisis period. This is consistent with Brehmer's (1987) argument that managers normally remember past experience.

Comparison between the older and younger managers regarding their perception of interest rate and foreign exchange risks showed a very interesting result. The less-experienced managers attributed higher priority to interest rate risk (42 per cent) while the more-experienced managers gave higher priority to foreign exchange risk (50 per cent). In the current period, there is a significant difference between managers experienced with their perception of interest rate risk. In particular, the less-experienced managers (50 per cent) gave higher priority to interest rate risk as compared with the more-experienced managers (19 per cent). This is arguably due to the fact that less-experienced managers are familiar with the interest rate futures made available by the Bursa Malaysia Derivative Bhd.

In terms of the extent of influence of ethnic group on managers, there is a significant difference between ethnic groups as regards to the perception of financial risks before the financial crisis and in the current period (Table 5.5). In the period before crisis, about 36 per cent of the Malay managers attributed greater importance to financial risks than did the Chinese managers (5 per cent). Similarly, in the current period, a majority (79 per cent) of Malay managers gave a higher priority to financial risks than did Chinese managers (53 per cent). This could be owing to the risk-averse culture of the Malays; another possible reason may be that Malay managers are still new to the business world (Gomez, 1999).

Types of foreign exchange exposure

The uncertainty of financial markets produces three types of foreign exchange exposure that require attention by multinationals, namely, transaction, translation, and economic exposures. According to Bodnar *et al.* (1996), economic exposure typically receives the least

Table 5.6 Short-term transaction exposure managed by ethnic Groups (before the crisis)

	0–25%	26–50%	51–75%	76–100%
Malay	14.3	29	36	21
Chinese	53	42	07	57

attention from multinationals, while transaction exposure is considered more important. However, Belk and Glaum (1990) showed that the UK multinationals started to give more consideration to translation exposure.

In the Malaysian context, about 29 per cent and 36 per cent of Malay managers managed from 26 per cent to 50 per cent and from 51 per cent to 75 per cent short-term transaction exposures, respectively, in the period before crisis (Table 5.6). In contrast, 53 per cent of the Chinese managed less than 25 per cent and 42 per cent managed between 26 per cent and 50 per cent for the same period. There is a significant difference in the management of these exposures between these two groups of managers (Table 5.7). The Malays seem to have managed more exposures than did their Chinese counterparts in the period before the crisis. During the crisis period, the percentage of Malay managers that managed more than 75 per cent of the short-term transaction exposures increased to 29 per cent while the percentage that managed between 51 per cent and 75 per cent remained the same. The percentage of the Chinese managers that managed between 51 per cent and 75 per cent increased dramatically from 0 to 37 per cent. In the current period, there remained a significant difference in foreign exchange risk management practices. The majority of Malay managers managed between 51 per cent and 75 per cent and from 76 per cent to 100 per cent of the short-term transaction exposures, while the Chinese were distributed from 0 per cent to 25 per cent, from 26 per cent to 50 per cent and from 51 per cent to 75 per cent. On the whole, the Malay managers appear to be more dependent on foreign exchange risk management than are the Chinese managers.

When we examined translation exposures, we found that both groups of managers managed the same amount of exposures in the period before the crisis (Table 5.7). However, during the crisis and for the current period, the Chinese managers managed more of these exposures than did the Malay managers. There is a significant

Table 5.7 Managers' traits and foreign exchange risk management practices – Kruskal–Wallis test

Type of exposure	Before crisis	During crisis	Current period
Transaction exposure less than a year (short-term)	**Ethnic Group** Chi-square – 9.091**** **Experience** Chi-square – 8.018** **Age** Chi-square – 7.399*	**Ethnic group** Chi-square – 2.053* **Age** Chi-square – 5.959*	**Ethnic group** Chi-square – 4.304***
Translation exposure	**Experience** Chi-square – 9.344***	**Ethnic group** Chi-square – 23.206**	**Ethnic group** Chi-square – 2.145* **Experience** Chi-square – 8.735**

* significant at 20%.
** significant at 10%.
*** significant at 5%.
**** significant at 1%.

difference between these two groups in managing these exposures (Table 5.7). One possible reason is a greater experience of Chinese managers (Gomez 1999).

Managing foreign exchange risk requires skill and experience, especially if managers decide to manage translation and economic exposures (Glaum 1990; Buckley 1996). Furthermore, Khim *et al.* (1997) argued that managing translation exposures in particular can be cumbersome because of the differences in accounting rules. Therefore, this study expects to find that managers' level of experience might have an influence on their foreign exchange risk management practices.

In the period before the crisis, the less-experienced managers were more involved in foreign exchange risk management by managing a greater amount of short-term transaction exposures than their more experienced counterparts (Table 5.7). Bukley (1996) argued that the lack of experience could be the reason for such behaviour, since managing short-term transactions is easier than managing other types of exposures. During the crisis period, owing to the volatility of the Malaysian dollar, most managers, irrespective of experience, did not want to take high risks and thus became more dependent on foreign exchange risk management.

Before the crisis, the more experienced managers managed a greater amount of translation exposures than the less-experienced ones (Table 5.7). Similarly, in the current period, perhaps owing to the hard lessons learned during the crisis, more experienced managers still managed a greater amount of these exposures. In contrast, the less experienced managers managed a lesser amount of translation exposures. These managers appear to be more interested in managing short-term transaction exposure. For obvious reasons, managers with more experience in foreign exchange risk management would be able to understand the mechanics of financial tools, and, therefore, arguably, would be more comfortable with currency management. Interestingly enough, the less experienced managers managed more short-term transaction exposures in the period before the crisis. This could be due to the greater priority given to currency exposure, and the fact that managing short-term transaction exposures is easier than managing translation exposures (Bukley 1996).

As expected, older managers managed a greater amount of transaction exposures in the period before crisis and during the crisis than younger ones (Table 5.7). This result is consistent with MacCrimmon and Wehrang (1990), who found that older managers are more conservative.

Foreign exchange risk management strategies

Oldfield and Santomero (1997) suggested that the management of risk can be classified into three strategies, which include risks that can be eliminated or avoided, risks that can be transferred to another party and risks that can be managed actively at company level. In the first of these risk strategies, risk avoidance is used to reduce the chances of idiosyncratic losses arising from a company's activities. Most managers would agree that risk cannot be controlled in such simple ways. In this study, approximately the same percentage of both Malays and Chinese would retreat from undertaking a project if the risk associated with it is significant (Table 5.8). There is no significant difference between the two ethnic groups of managers in relation to this issue (Table 5.9).

The second risk strategy is a method more commonly employed by multinationals. Risk associated with payment in foreign currencies can be reduced by relying on financial instruments, such as forwards, futures, options and swaps. The markets for these instruments have

Table 5.8 Managers' ethnic groups and foreign exchange risk management strategies

	Percentage agreed	
Strategy	**Malays**	**Chinese**
Aware of risks and retreat	21.4	21.1
Aware of risks and hedge all	28.6	5.3
Aware of risks and hedge depending on amount of losses and cost to hedge	8.6	94.7
Aware of risks and hedge if there is a high chance of losses regardless of cost	21.4	0.0

Table 5.9 Managers' ethnic groups and foreign exchange risk management strategies – Kruskal–Wallis test

	Chi-square value
Aware of risks and retreat	1.849*
Aware of risks and hedge all	8.014****
Aware of risks and hedge depending on amount of losses and cost to hedge	2.626*
Aware of risks and hedge if there is a high chance of losses regardless of cost	3.613**

* significant at 20%.
** significant at 10%.
**** significant at 1%.

grown rapidly in the last two decades. In the study, the majority (94 per cent) of managers who engaged in foreign exchange risk management used forward contracts, while 53 per cent of them used swap (Table 5.10). It can be argued that many managers became involved with forward contracts because they are easily understood and widely available from local banks. Meanwhile, the percentage involved with options and futures was small, that is 29 per cent and 6 per cent, respectively. These findings are consistent with Khim and Liang's (1997) study of Singaporean companies where 83 per cent used forward contracts while 43 per cent used swaps. On the contrary, Khim's study also found that 83 per cent of the Singaporean companies used future contracts. This differs from the results of our study, but it is not surprising, given that there is only one type of future contract available to multinationals in Malaysia under the Bursa Malaysia Derivative Bhd.

Table 5.10 Importance of financial tools in foreign exchange risk management

Financial tool	Percentage of importance
Forward	94.1
Swap	52.9
Option	29.4
Future	5.8

It is interesting to note that about 93 per cent of Malay managers said they would buy forward contracts in order to manage known future payments. Similarly, about 90 per cent of the Chinese managers would do so. Therefore, it suggests that both groups of managers were unwilling to expose themselves to currency risk. On the other hand, both groups of managers were willing to take greater risks with regard to future currency receipts. Only half of the two groups of managers were involved in forward contracts to mitigate future currency receipts. Thus, it could be argued that some managers were willing to 'gamble' on favourable currency rates.

The third of Oldfield and Santomero's strategies, inherent risks arising from business operations, can be actively managed. This involves an integrated risk management programme, starting from risk identification, risk quantification until implementation and monitoring of the programme (Baldoni 1998; Rahardjo and Dowling 1998).

Managers who actively manage foreign exchange risk can mitigate risk by using financial tools. In this study, few managers stated that they would hedge all currency exposures regardless of cost. Specifically, Table 5.8 shows that about 29 per cent of the Malay managers and only 5 per cent of the Chinese hedged all exposure regardless of costs. There is a significant difference between these two groups of managers on this issue. Rodriguez (1980) would classify managers who seek to hedge all risks as risk-paranoid. In this study, the Malay managers could be considered as more risk-paranoid than Chinese managers.

From Table 5.8, about 95 per cent of the Chinese and 79 per cent of the Malay managers would have hedged currency exposures, given that the costs of managing these exposures were less than the expected losses. Table 5.9 indicates a significant difference between these two groups of managers, with Chinese managers more likely to hedge currency exposures if the costs of hedging are less than the expected losses. Following Rodriguez (1980), this group of managers would be referred to as risk-neutral. Our study suggested that the Chinese managers were more risk-neutral than the Malays.

Again, Rodriguez (1980) categorized managers who would manage risks regardless of cost, if those risks are likely to result in losses, as risk-asymmetric. Table 5.8 shows that 22 per cent of the Malay managers and none of the Chinese managers would have hedged regardless of costs, had exposures been likely to result in losses. As shown in Table 5.9, there was a significant difference between these two groups of managers, with by Malay managers found to be more risk-asymmetric than Chinese.

Views on the direction of foreign exchange rates and hedging

As mentioned in the previous section, forecasting the direction of foreign exchange rates is important because it may influence managers' decisions on the management of foreign exchange risk. For example, if the expected movements of the exchange rates are favourable, managers are better off to absorb the risks at firm level and vice versa. Madura (2000) argued that forecasting exchange rates is necessary for a number of reasons which may influence multinationals' decision-making. Currency rate forecasting may influence hedging decisions, short-term financing decisions, short-term investment decisions, capital budgeting decisions, long-term financing decisions and earning assessments. For example, a multinational which has to pay in pounds sterling in three months for imported goods may decide not to hedge currency exposure if the pound is forecast as weakening during that period. Therefore, if the expected exchange rate is favourable, most probably multinationals do not have to manage currency risk, or perhaps need manage only a small amount. On the other hand, if the exchange is expected to be unfavourable, they can manage more of the risk.

The results of this study showed that about 10 per cent of managers who had forecast exchange rates managed 100 per cent of the currency exposure as compared to only 5 per cent for those who did not forecast. On the whole, managers who had forecast the direction of foreign exchange rates managed more exposure as compared to those who did not (Tables 5.11 and 5.12). On average, those who did forecast the exchange rates managed about 61 per cent of the exposure as compared with 34.7 per cent of those who did not. In one exceptional case, a manager did not forecast the direction of foreign exchange rates but decided to manage 100 per cent of the exposure. A total of 45.3 per cent of the managers managed more than 60 per cent of the currency exposure if they had views on the direction of foreign exchange rates, while only 4.3 per cent managed the same amount of exposure if they had no views. Thus, in general, managers felt more comfortable about engaging in foreign risk management practices when they had views on the direction of currency rates. This was because managers in Malaysian multinationals used risk management for hedging purposes, not for speculative ones. This result differs from that in Dolde's (1993) study of US large firms, where a higher percentage of the US firms managed currency exposure if they had no views. In particular, Dolde's study found that about 44 per cent of US firms managed more than 60 per cent of currency exposure if they had no views on the foreign exchange rates. In addition, Dolde's study showed that about 53 per cent of US firms managed more than 60 per cent of currency exposure when they had views on the foreign exchange movements. Dolde's results implied that these multinationals are biased toward offsetting risks. When the views were favourable they would hedge less of the currency exposure.

On examination of managers' ethnic groups, about 17 per cent of the Malay managers were found to have managed 100 per cent of the currency exposure, as compared with only 6 per cent of the Chinese when they held views on exchange rates. When managers had views on the exchange rates, the majority (67 per cent) of the Malay

Table 5.11 Currency exposure managed by managers who forecast foreign exchange rates and hedging

Percentage managed	Percentage of multinationals
0–20	3.2
21–40	6.4
41–60	45.1
61–80	25.9
81–100	19.4
Total	100

Table 5.12 Currency exposure managed by managers who did not forecast foreign exchange rate and hedging

Percentage managed	Percentage of multinationals
0–20	26.1
21–40	34.8
41–60	34.8
61–80	0.0
81–100	4.3
Total	100

managers managed 50 per cent of the exposure compared with 33 per cent of the Chinese. If managers had no views on exchange rates, about 13 per cent of the Malays managed 100 per cent of the exposure, compared with none of the Chinese. Without views, 63 per cent of the Malays managed 50 per cent of currency exposure compared with 21 per cent of the Chinese. The Chinese managed less currency exposure if they had no view on the direction of exchange rates and vice versa. The results imply that Chinese managers were involved in foreign exchange risk management only if they had knowledge of the direction of exchange rates. On the other hand, the majority of the Malay managers seemed to be dependent on risk management irrespective whether or not they had views on the direction of foreign exchange rates. These results reaffirm earlier findings that Malay managers were risk-paranoid and risk-asymmetric while the Chinese managers were risk-neutral.

Conclusion

This chapter describes how managers' traits may influence their perceptions and practices in foreign exchange risk management. Several important findings relating to these isses include the following:

1. Malay managers perceived greater priority to financial risks, especially foreign exchange risk;
2. Malay managers managed more currency risk compared with Chinese managers, irrespective of their views on foreign exchange rates;

3. Malay managers could be categorized as risk-paranoid and risk-asymmetrical, the Chinese as risk-neutral;
4. older managers managed more currency risks, thus they were more risk averse than the younger managers;
5. managers with less experience in the management of foreign exchange risks managed a greater amount of short-term transaction exposure, while the more experienced managed a greater amount of translation exposure;
6. managing short-term transaction exposures is more popular among Malaysian managers.

Overall, these findings support the assumptions made and in some ways are consistent with earlier studies in developed countries.

This study also indicates that foreign exchange risk management seems to have become more popular among Malaysian multinationals, especially during the crisis period. Thus, the role of foreign exchange risk management is becoming more important in the Malaysian corporate world.

References

Abdullah, A. (1996) *Going Global: Cultural Dimensions In Malaysian Management*. Kuala Lumpur: Malaysian Institute of Management.

Ankrom, R.K. (1974) 'Top-Level Approach to the Foreign Exchange Problem', *Harvard Business Review*, 52(3), 79–90.

Baldoni, R.J.A. (1998) 'Best Practices Approach to Risk Management', *TMA Journal*, 18(1), 30–4.

Belk, P.A. and M. Glaum (1990) 'The Management of Foreign Exchange Risk in UK Multinationals: An Empirical Investigation', *Accounting and Business Research*, 21(18), 3–13.

Berkman, H. and M.E. Bradbury (1996) 'Empirical Evidence on the Corporate Use of Derivatives', *Financial Management*, 25(2), 5–13.

Bodnar, G.M., G.S. Hayt, and R.C. Marstan (1998), A 1998 Wharton Survey of Derivatives by US Non-Financial Firms, *Financial Management*, 27(winter), 70–91.

Brehmer, B. (1987) *Psychology of Risk* in Singleton, W.T. and J. Hovden (eds.), *Risk and Decisions*, New York: Wiley, and Sons, pp. 25–39.

Bukley, P.J. and M.C. Casson (1985) *The Economic Theory of The Multinational Enterprise*. London: Macmillan.

Bukley, A. (1996) *Multinational Finance*, 3rd edition, London, New York, Prentice Hall.

Chiu, D. and S. Foerster (1997) 'Using Derivatives to Manage Risk', *Ivey Business Quarterly*, 61(3), 56–64.

Dolde, W. (1993) 'The Trajectory of Corporate Financial Risk Management', *Journal of Applied Corporate Finance*, 6: 33–41.
Douglas, M. and A. Wildavsky (1982) *Risk and Culture*. Berkeley: University of California Press.
Froot, K.A., D.S. Schartein and J.C. Stein (1994) 'A Framework for Risk Management', *Harvard Business Review*, Nov-Dec 1994, 91–102.
Geczy, C., B.A. Minton and C.M. Schoard (1997) 'Why Firms Use Currency Derivatives', *Journal of Finance*, 52(4), 1323–54.
Glaum, M. (1990) 'Strategic Management of Exchange Rate Risks', *Long Range Planning*, 23(4), 65–72.
Gomez, E.T. (1999) *Chinese Business in Malaysia*. Surrey: Curzon Press.
Joseph, N.L. and R.D. Hewins (1997) 'The Motives for Corporate Hedging among UK Multinationals'. *International Journal of Finance and Economic*, vol. 2, 151–71.
Khim, E.M. and D.L.K. Liang (1997) 'The Use of Derivatives Financial Instruments in Company Financial Risk Management: The Singapore Experience', *Singapore Management Review*, 19(2), 17–44.
MacCrimmon, K.R. and D.A. Wehrung (1990) 'Characteristics of Risk taking Executives', *Management Science*, 36(APHP), 422–35.
Madura, J. (2000) *International Financial Management*, 6th edition, South Western, New York.
Makar, S.D. and S.P. Huffman (1997) 'Foreign Exchange Risk Management Practices in U.S. Multinationals', *Journal of Applied Business Research*, 13(2), 73–86.
Malindretos, J. and D. Tsanacas (1995) 'Hedging Preferences and Foreign Exchange Exposure Management', *Multinational Business Review*, 3(2), 56–66.
New Straits Times (1998) 'Urgent Need for Local Firms to Enhance Risk Management', *New Straits Times*, 20 January 1998, page B3, Kuala Lumpur.
Oldfield, G.S. and A.M. Santomero (1997) 'Risk Management in Financial Institutions', *Sloan Management Review*, 39(1), 33–46.
Rahardjo, K. and M.A. Dowling (1998) 'A Broader Vision: Strategic Risk Management', *Risk Management*, 45(9), 44–50.
Rodriguez, R.M. (1980) *Foreign Exchange Management in U.S. Multinationals*. Lexington, MA: Lexington.
Saunders, M., P. Lewis, *et al.*(1997) *Research Methods for Business Students*. London: Pitman.
Smithson, C.W., Clifford W. Smith *et al.* (eds) (1995) *Managing Financial Risk – A Guide to Derivative Products, Financial Engineering, and Value Maximization*. Irwin, IL: Barr Ridge.
Vaus, D.A.D. (1993) *Surveys In Social Research*. London: University College of London Press.
Wallace, J. (1998) 'Best Practices in Foreign Exchange Risk Management', *TMA Journal*, 18(6), 48–55.

6
Foreign Direct Investment in North Africa: A Comparative Perspective

Ahmed Aghrout and Michael Hodd

Introduction

The North African countries (Algeria, Morocco and Tunisia) have, since the early 1980s, embarked upon important reforms aimed at restructuring their economies via liberalization and privatization, but with varying degrees and pace across the region. Like many other developing countries, they have found that the difficulties engendered by the economic policies pursued, and the poor performance associated with decades of state-led development, have left them with no alternative other than to engage in a process of reforms at a time when the world economy was undergoing major transformations.

The move towards a market-oriented economy is being perceived as crucial to rapid economic growth. Given the difficulties encountered in obtaining foreign aid and loans, and the problems they generate in terms of debt, other sources have to be found to support this transitional phase. In this context, the North African countries have made foreign private investment one major source of financing their development process. The programme of reforms implemented and under way, is, among other things, expected to provide a favourable environment and an attractive location for private foreign capital, particularly in the form of foreign direct investment (FDI).

Considering the main policy measures undertaken by the governments concerned, this chapter seeks to assess the degree of their success in bolstering FDI inflows into the region. First, we describe succinctly some of the main institutional and regulatory innovations introduced to enhance the attractiveness of their markets for this type of investment. Next, we provide a balance sheet of their respective performances on the basis of recent FDI statistical trends both within the region and in relation to countries of more or less comparable levels of development. A number of issues are raised that need to be addressed in order to improve the enabling environment intended for businesses to expand and diversify in this region.

Finally we examine the evidence for the spillover impact of FDI on economic performance in the three countries, particularly the contention that FDI and human resource development are complementary in their impact, and that a minimum level of human resource development is necessary for the significant spillover effects from FDI to occur.

Policy framework

Before reviewing the region's endeavour to improve its investment climate, it is worth taking quick look at the rationale behind the growing importance of FDI as a major source of foreign investment. The proliferation of an abundant theoretical and empirical literature about the implications of FDI on growth has contributed to changing the long-held negative perception of this source of investment, particularly in developing countries. Indeed, during the 1960s and 1970s multinational corporations were often regarded as a means of foreign economic domination. Yet this perception has changed considerably in the last two decades, being replaced by a generally optimistic view of the benefits to the host countries. For many developing countries the debt crisis of the 1980s has, since then, made loans hard to come by. Given this constraint and the low level of domestic savings, foreign private investment, especially in the form of FDI, has become an attractive source of foreign capital.

Numerous studies have dealt with the implications of FDI on the recipient countries, ranging from broader effects such as growth to specific impacts on sectoral issues such as trade, technology, employment and so forth (see Borensztein *et al.* 1995; Moran 1998). By and large, FDI is expected to contribute to the growth of host economies through the following:

- an increase in the quantity of physical capital, and a rise in its quality through technology transfer;

- the development of managerial skills and employment;
- the promotion of different types of linkages with local companies, stimulating local productivity through backward linkages to domestic service suppliers;
- the development of niche export markets.

In relation to the last contributing factor, UNCTAD (2002) contended that:

> TNCs [transnational corporations] play an important role in the exports of many developing countries and economies in transition. Indeed, for the most dynamic products in world trade, TNCs are central for enabling these countries to reach world markets, and they provide some of the 'missing elements' that developing countries need to upgrade their competitiveness in export markets.

It is this context that prompted the North African governments to make efforts to improve their investment climate with a view to benefiting from the advantages associated with this source of capital (for a detailed accounts of host country determinants of FDI see UNCTAD 1998; Colton 1999; Mallampally and Sauvant 1999). To promote the conditions conducive to an investment-friendly environment, the countries concerned introduced legislation providing the institutional and legal frameworks for regulating foreign investment. Establishing investment promotion agencies became one vital policy measure in this undertaking. These structures were set up in the 1990s – the National Investment Promotion Agency (ANDI) in 2001 in Algeria, the Direction of Investments (DI) in 1996 in Morocco and the Foreign Investment Promotion Agency (FIPA) in 1995 in Tunisia. In general, these agencies are entrusted with the key missions of policy advocacy, image-building, investor-servicing and investment generation (ANIMA 2004a). They are now involved in the ANIMA project – the Euro-Mediterranean Network of Investment Promotion Agencies – launched in September 2002, associating the European Union (EU) and the 12 Mediterranean partner countries (MED-12). The project's overall aim is to increase FDI in the Mediterranean via efficient cooperation between both parties, particularly through institutional support to the EU partners' investment promotion agencies, networking and the establishment of a knowledge base on the region's investment opportunities (ANIMA 2002).

Efforts have also targeted the regulatory regimes to make them more liberal and investor-friendly (Tunisia 1994, Morocco 1995, Algeria 2001). At the national level, legislation in Algeria, Morocco and Tunisia now offers a wide range of incentives such as tax breaks, non-discrimination and identical treatment between foreign and domestic investors, protection against expropriation, recourse to international arbitration and guarantees to transfer profit and capital. Further incentives are granted to investment projects in sectors and/or geographical zones considered by the relevant authorities to be of 'special importance' (Tunisia 2004). Except for certain areas (so-called sensitive sectors), foreign investors can invest freely in virtually all sectors. For instance, the respective investment promotion agencies have identified a number of key sectors with investment potential:

- Algeria (agriculture, fishing and agro-food, hydraulics, building and construction, transport and infrastructure, banking and insurance, telecommunications, energy, and health and pharmaceutical products);
- Morocco (agriculture, distribution, energy, high-technology industries, textiles, tourism, transport and water);
- Tunisia (electricals and electronics, food processing, pharmaceuticals, telecommunications and tourism, textiles and leather) (ANIMA 2004a).

Various types of investment are offered. In Algeria, for instance, these are as follows:

- asset acquisition (creation of new activities, capacity extension, rehabilitation, and restructuring);
- capital participation in public companies (cash contributions and contribution in kind);
- privatization of public companies (partial privatization and total privatization) (ANIMA 2004a).

All things considered, the new investment regimes lifted many of the prevailing restrictions on FDI entry (screening requirements and other restrictions) and the operation of branches and affiliates (UNCTAD 2000). While noteworthy progress has been achieved, there is still room for improvement. Indeed, a recent and comprehensive

Table 6.1 Starting a business in North Africa

	Procedures (no.)	Duration (days)	Cost (% of GNP per capita)	Minimum capital (% of GNI per capita)
Algeria	18	29	31.9	73.0
Morocco	11	36	19.1	762.5
Tunisia	10	46	16.4	351.7
MENA*	11	50	54.5	1,104.3
OECD**	6	30	10.2	61.2

* Average in the Middle East and North Africa.
** Average in OECD.

Source: Based on data derived from World Bank (2004).

study on business environment in 133 countries conducted by the World Bank makes it clear that the North African countries need to make further changes to their enabling investment environment. Table 6.1 gives an idea about the challenges to setting up a business in these countries, using a number of measures. For instance, there are on average 13 administrative procedures required, an associated time and cost of 37 days and 367 dollars respectively, and 396 per cent minimum capital required (as a percentage of GNI per capita). Clearly, between these countries there are variations but, as a group, they seem to be in a better position in relation to the MENA region as whole. Nevertheless, comparing their investment climate (main indicators for starting a business) with that of the OECD – or even an emerging market such as Malaysia – more work needs to be done, at least in terms of simplifying procedures and reducing time and costs.

FDI indicators

Table 6.2 shows that World FDI flows (inward) declined to US$651.2bn in 2002 after attaining a record level of US$1393bn in 2000. This downturn started from 2001, corresponding to a flow of US$823.8bn (UNCTAD 2003). The share of developing countries, which was on average about US$50bn per year during the period 1985–95, increased to nearly US$246.0bn in 2000, but went down to US$162.1bn in 2002, that is nearly 25 per cent of the total (UNCTAD 2003). In short, as Figure 6.1 reveals, one possible reason why the

Table 6.2 FDI inflows into Algeria, Morocco and Tunisia (US$bn)

	1985–95 (annual average)	1998	2000	2001	2002
Algeria	0.017	0.501	0.438	1.196	1.065
Morocco	0.237	0.417	0.423	2.808	0.428
Tunisia	0.260	0.668	0.779	0.486	0.821
Developing countries	50.0	191.3	246.1	209.4	162.1
World	181.0	686.0	1,393.0	824.0	651.2

Source: UNCTAD (2003).

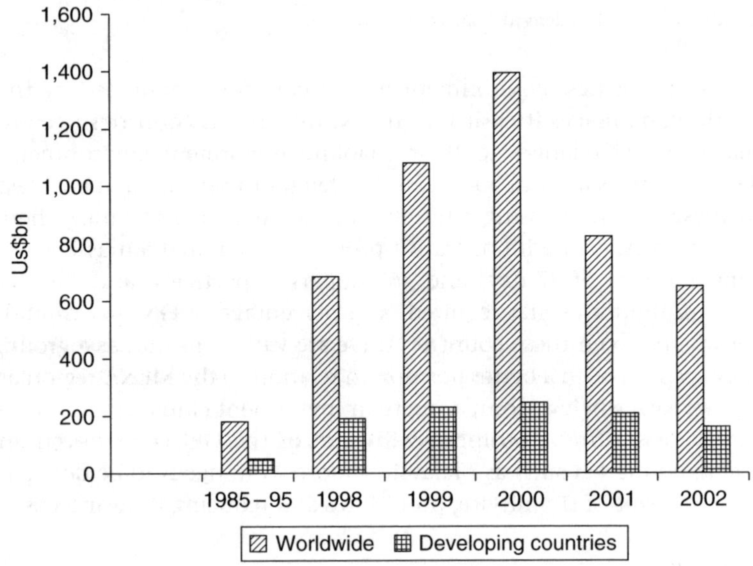

Figure 6.1 FDI flows: worldwide and developing countries
Source: Based on data derived from UNCTAD (2003).

developing countries have not fared well in recent years is a global downward trend.

In spite of the fact that Algeria, Morocco and Tunisia are striving to attract FDI, they remain one of the less attractive zones when compared with other regions. By way of illustration, their share of FDI flows to developing countries and economies, as a group, was 1.4 per cent

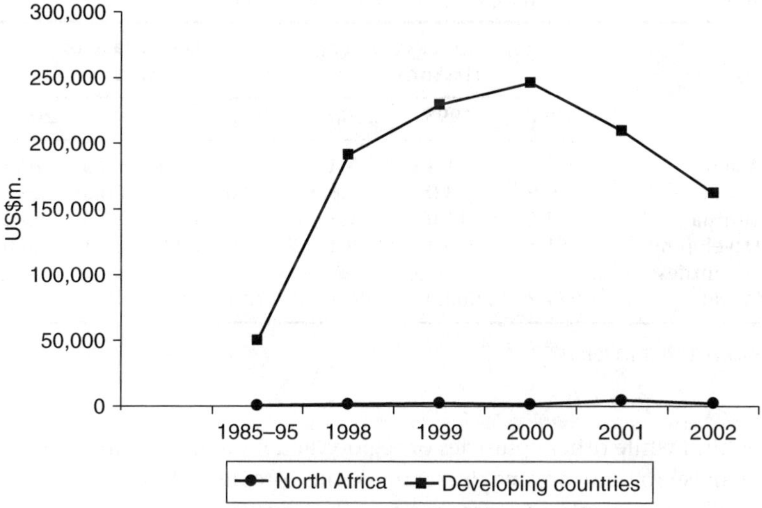

Figure 6.2 FDI flows to North Africa and developing countries
Source: Based on data derived from UNCTAD (2003).

in 2002, a proportion well below the 2.1 per cent exceptional level in 2001 (Figure 6.2). A clear picture can be obtained by looking at their individual performance. Table 6.2 shows that the North African countries have witnessed fluctuating levels of FDI inflows, occasionally reaching their highest point (Algeria in 2001 and 2002, and Morocco in 2001). Except for these recent increases, FDI flows to Algeria in particular remain modest, if not small in an economy considered one of the largest in Africa. It is not surprising then to notice that the FDI stocks vary greatly across the North African region.

As Table 6.3 reveals, inflows by absolute values and stocks show a steady increase, but may not provide a much clearer elucidation of the importance of inward FDI for the host country or countries. Therefore the attractiveness of a country can be appreciated by looking at how significant is the ratio of FDI to GDP. The same table provides an indication of the importance of this ratio in the region's economies. Over time, this shows no significant change, reflecting the region's low attractiveness. This is chiefly the case for Algeria compared with its immediate neighbours and the developing countries as a whole. Recording a ratio of 10.5 per cent in 2002, Algeria is still lagging far

Table 6.3 FDI stocks in Algeria, Morocco and Tunisia

	Stocks (US$bn)				Percentage of GDP		
	1990	1995	2000	2002	1990	2000	2002
Algeria	1.4	1.4	3.4	5.7	2.2	6.5	10.5
Morocco	0.9	3.0	6.8	10.0	3.5	20.3	26.9
Tunisia	7.6	11.0	11.5	14.0	62.0	59.3	66.2
Developing countries	551.5	920.4	2,029.4	2,340.0	14.8	31.1	36.0
World	1,954.2	3,002.0	6,146.7	7,122.4	9.3	19.6	22.3

Source: UNCTAD (2003).

behind while other countries or regions at a more or less similar level of development are making remarkable inroads – Morocco almost 27 per cent, Tunisia 66 per cent and the developing countries 36 per cent. The marginal role played by FDI in Algeria is quite evident when we take into consideration the FDI impact on gross fixed capital formation. Between 1999 and 2002, the FDI contribution was 6.2 per cent, whereas Morocco registered 16 per cent, Tunisia just about 12 per cent, and the average in developing countries was more than 13 per cent (UNCTAD 2003).

No doubt all these indicators suggest that Algeria needs to make much more effort to improve its image as a good location for business and private investment. However, it should be borne in mind that reforms undertaken in Morocco and Tunisia, especially in relation to privatization, progressed at a faster pace than in Algeria. Indeed, the privatization programme did contribute to increasing the FDI inflows in these countries. During the period 1990–9, proceeds from privatization amounted to US$3102m. in Morocco, US$523m. in Tunisia and only US$55.1m. in Algeria (World Bank 2001). It should be noted that, for comparability, these figures for Algeria do not include those investments in the hydrocarbon sector (exploration and production sharing). There are 20 foreign oil companies operating in Algeria, with US$2.5bn invested in exploration (Sonatrach 2002). Investment in this sector increased from US$671m. in 1999 to US$2.3bn in 2003, and the cumulated stock amounted to US$8.6 bn over the period 1999–2003 (Algérie Presse Service 2004).

It is the case that FDI inflows into the region remain focused on certain economic sectors. In Algeria the energy sector has so far attracted most of the FDI, with the remainder going to a few other sectors such as telecommunications and steel. Over the period 1993–2002, 42 per cent of FDI went to the telecommunications sector, 17 per cent to the food, electrical and electronic industry, and 11 per cent to the banking sector in Morocco (Morocco 2004). Until the end of 1997 foreign investment, outside the energy sector, did not rise much in Tunisia. However, after that date the manufacturing industries increased their share of FDI, reaching 36 per cent in 2003 compared with 40 per cent and 17 per cent in the energy and service sectors respectively. In Tunisia, FDI represents 10 per cent of productive investment and generates one-third of exports and one-sixth of total employment (Tunisia 2004).

Another way of appraising the relative importance of FDI flows into these countries is by comparing flows with performance within the Euro-Mediterranean zone. The three countries are signatories to the EU association agreements, as part of Europe's partnership policy, launched during the Euro-Mediterranean Conference on 27–28 November 1995 in Barcelona (Aghrout 2000). The declaration adopted stated that 'economic development must be supported both by internal savings, the basis of investment, and by direct foreign investment', and emphasis was put on 'the importance of creating an environment conducive to investment, in particular the progressive elimination of obstacles to such investment which could lead to the transfer of technology and increase in production and exports' (European Commission 1995).

The North African countries have been placing high hopes on their partnership arrangements with the EU. For instance, the targeted growth rate of 8 per cent a year expected by Morocco from the agreement is based in large part on attracting foreign direct investment (*Financial Times* 1995b). In like manner for Tunisia, it has been argued that unless it can attract US$1bn of new foreign direct investment per year in all sectors, then its free-trade deal with the EU will be detrimental to its economy (*Arabies* 1995). While these initial expectations may not have materialized in practice, they do however reflect the significance attached to this type of investment in integrating the North African economies into the European economic environment.

According to available statistics, FDI flows (registered capital and other transactions) from the EU to the MED-12 increased from €0.444bn in 1992 to €2.350bn in 2001, a level still relatively low in comparison with the EU's commitment in other parts of the world such as the candidate countries, the Mercosur countries and the Asian NICs (Eurostat 2003). Over this period, the North African countries' share has risen from 7 per cent to 21 per cent, reflecting a much more significant position of the EU's FDI in the region (Morocco and Tunisia in particular) in recent years. However, a more detailed picture of European investment in the region is provided by a recent report (2003) from the Euro-Mediterranean Network of Investment Promotion Agencies (referred to under the acronym of ANIMA), which considers that the 'region's attractiveness is improving' (ANIMA 2004b). Accordingly, its analysis of investments by sub-region of destination in 2003 shows the following:

- Maghreb (Algeria, Morocco, Tunisia): 146 projects (53 per cent);
- Machrek (Egypt, Jordan, Lebanon, Palestine, Syria): 52 projects (19 per cent);
- Other Mediterranean countries (Cyprus, Israel, Malta, Turkey): 77 projects (28 per cent).

With about 162 projects (59 per cent), the EU occupies a relatively dominant position as a source of FDI flows to the MED-12, followed by the USA (44 projects, 16 per cent) and Islamic countries (19 projects, 7 per cent) (ANIMA 2004b). While the predominance of the North African region is evident – accounting for more than a half of the MED-12 total, 275 projects – it is the case that other regions such as Central and Eastern Europe have performed much better, as they were the destination of 451 FDI projects during the same period of time (2003). Obviously, this performance can be explained by the fact many countries in this region are new candidates, having joined the EU in May this year.

FDI impact

Borensztein *et al.* (1995) have argued that FDI makes a contribution to economic growth in excess of the impact that would be expected from the addition it makes to the capital stock. As mentioned earlier, these contributions come from spillovers of technology, development of skills, managerial improvements and so on. One interesting feature of the results of Borensztein *et al.* is that they argue that it is necessary to have a minimum level of skill capacity in the labour force in order to benefit from the spillovers from FDI.

Borensztein *et al.* examine economic performance in a group of 69 developing countries. They seek to explain differences in GDP per head growth rates by indicators reflecting capital accumulation, labour skill levels, the income gap with the high-income countries (reflecting the ease at which technology can be upgraded), the size of the government sector, the degree of economic liberalization and the extent of FDI inflows. FDI flows on their own, however, do not appear to be significantly related to growth in GDP per head. The impact of FDI depends on the level of human resource development: the higher the level of skills, the greater the impact of a given level of FDI.

Borensztein *et al.* go on to argue that there is a threshold level of human resource development which needs to be achieved before the spillovers from FDI begin to be realized. In the absence of the threshold level of skills, FDI tends to operate in enclaves, operated by expatriates. Above the threshold level, local workers are employed, mastering enhanced skills and technology which they then take into the wider economy.

The indicator used by Borensztein *et al.* is the enrolment rate in secondary education, and their work suggests that a 52 per cent enrolment rate is required before FDI really begins to generate significant spillovers.

The empirical work is related to average economic performance averaged over two decades, 1970–9 and 1980–9, and with 69 countries involved, there are 138 observations in the cross-section study. As is usual in such studies, the explanatory variables employed explain a small part (at best only 40 per cent) of the differences in growth of GDP per head observed. While we acknowledge there is a way to go in terms of having a comprehensive explanation of economic performance, the spirit of such studies is to try to identify factors that appear to have a strong influence on the growth process. The complimentary influence of human resource development and FDI would appear to be one such factor identified by this study.

Data on the years 1973 to 1993 for the three North African economies that are the focus of this chapter are assembled in Tables 6.4, 6.6 and 6.8. Looking at the average figures over the period, Tunisia has had the strongest growth of GDP per head (2.3 per cent p.a.), followed by Morocco (1.9 per cent p.a.), with Algeria (0.1 per cent p.a.) being the weakest. This corresponds to the ranking FDI inflows in relation to overall investment, with FDI 5.2 per cent of investment in Tunisia, 2.7 per cent in Morocco and 0.7 per cent in Algeria.

All three countries have improved their educational provision in the period. In terms of the indicator employed by Borensztein *et al.*, that is secondary school enrolments, Algeria has done best, raising enrolment ratios from 14 per cent to 60 per cent, followed by Tunisia (19 per cent to 43 per cent) and Morocco (14 per cent to 28 per cent). Algeria is the only country with levels of the indicator above the threshold of 52 per cent suggested by Borensztein *et al.*

The data were assembled to try to test over time the hypothesis on complimentarity of human resource development and FDI for each of the three countries in the region. A dummy variable for the introduction of economic liberalization programmes is used instead of the parallel market rate for foreign exchange used by Borensztein *et al.*, but otherwise the variables are the same. A lag of two years is assumed for the impact of FDI to show up in the growth of GDP per head.

Some preliminary regression results for each country are presented in Tables 6.5, 6.7 and 6.9. The sign of various variables here are the same as those used by Borensztein *et al.* as explanatory factor. The only variable which consistently exhibited the hypothesized sign (but which was only significant at the 5 per cent level for Tunisia) was the share of the government sector. The complementarity of FDI and human resource development in determining economic growth does not show up strongly in the results. The direction of the causal link is as expected for Tunisia and Algeria (but not Morocco), and the results are not significant. This is not entirely unexpected – it is usually difficult to observe patterns established in a cross-section study showing up strongly in a time-series study.

This work is at a preliminary stage. It is expected that the data period can be extended, enabling a better analysis of the time series properties (some of the variables are clearly not stationary, and some probably are), and the extra information will improve the possibility of generating more decisive results.

Concluding remarks

It is apparent that the North African countries, in their reform programmes, have endeavoured to create conditions (legal, institutional and other) that will make their region an attractive location, especially for FDI inflows. The extent and the pace of the policy reforms have varied across the region. It is also the case that the FDI flows have tended to fluctuate from year to year and within the region, and from country to country. Nevertheless, these flows remain relatively low when compared with other emerging markets. For instance, the EU experts have estimated the investment potential in the Algerian market at US$8bn per year. This country, according to them, is losing between US$5bn and US$6bn in FDI flows each year, despite the high levels registered between 2001 and 2002.

The persistence of a number of obstacles needs to be addressed in an efficient and forward-looking way. Among these one can cite the absence of a larger market, the still existing regulatory hurdles, political and security uncertainties, and the slow process of privatization. The latter issue is and continues to be an important component of the reform programme, but has not progressed at the desired pace, notably in Algeria and to a lesser extent in Morocco. Nonetheless, one should bear in mind the fact that privatization has, with the exception of the hydrocarbon sector, been the main contributor to the FDI inflows in these countries – for instance, the sale of licences in the telecommunications sector in Algeria and Morocco.

For some time to come, the importance of foreign financing in the form of FDI promises to be extremely important in smoothing the region's transitional process towards a market economy, in its relations with the EU, and in the commitment to multilateral trade liberalization. It is clear that increasing FDI flows requires not only the diversifying of its sectoral focus, but promoting its activities in 'greenfield' areas as well.

Evidence on the spillover impact of FDI in the region is not strongly evident, particularly the nature of the complementarity of human resource development and FDI, and more work remains to be done here.

Appendix

Table 6.4 Algeria: data

Year	GDP/ head growth (% p.a.) (GHG)	Sec. sch. enr't (%) (SSE)	Sec. sch. enr't dummy (SCD)	Govt/ GDP (%) (GOP)	Inv./ GDP (%) (INP)	FDI/ Inv. (%) (FDP)	Economic reform dummy (REF)	FDI × SSE (F × S)
1973	4.0	14	0	11.8	35.9	1.6	0	22.35
1974	−10.0	17	0	14.4	45.2	6.0	0	101.36
1975	2.6	20	0	16.2	46.8	1.2	0	23.32
1976	4.5	23	0	15.6	44.5	2.3	0	53.38
1977	1.1	27	0	15.2	49.7	1.7	0	44.68
1978	5.7	29	0	14.4	54.6	0.9	0	27.12
1979	4.8	31	0	17.4	47.2	0.1	0	1.99
1980	−3.3	33	0	16.8	47.9	1.5	0	51.14
1981	−1.1	36	0	17.4	48.2	0.0	0	−0.24
1982	3.6	39	0	17.4	45.4	−0.3	0	−12.33
1983	3.4	43	0	17.5	45.8	−0.1	0	−2.65
1984	1.7	47	0	17.6	44.1	−0.1	0	−2.78
1985	4.0	50	0	17.5	42.8	0.0	0	−0.41
1986	−1.6	53	1	18.4	36.6	−0.3	0	−14.71
1987	−2.5	54	1	18.5	30.0	−0.1	0	−3.15
1988	−4.3	61	1	19.9	31.9	0.0	0	2.01
1989	1.4	61	1	19.3	33.1	0.0	1	1.31
1990	−5.7	60	1	20.2	31.6	0.0	1	−1.39
1991	−4.3	60	1	22.3	27.4	−0.3	1	−18.51
1992	0.8	60	1	24.1	25.5	0.0	1	1.47
1993	−2.3	60	1	24.3	23.7	0.0	1	−1.02
Average	0.1	42		17.9	39.9	0.7		

GHG = GDP per head, growth rate, % p.a.
SSE = secondary school enrolment rate, % of 12–17 age group.
SCD = dummy variable, 1 when SSE ≥ 52%, 0 otherwise.
GOP = ratio of government expenditure to GDP (%).
INP = ratio of investment to GDP (%).
FDP = ratio of foreign direct investment to investment (%).
REF = economic reform dummy variable, 0 for 1973–88, 1 for 1989–93.
F × S = FDI × SSE.

Sources: World Bank, *World Tables* (various issues); IMF, *International Financial Statistics* (various issues).

Table 6.5 Algeria: growth, government size and skill levels

Dependent variable: GHG.
Method: least squares.
Sample (adjusted): 1975–1993.
Included observations: 19 after adjusting endpoints.

Variable	Coefficient	Standard error	*t*-statistic	Probability
C	7.713737	5.986228	1.288581	0.2159
GOP	−0.428021	0.309395	−1.383414	0.1855
F × S(−2)	0.043107	0.028168	1.530350	0.1455
R^2	0.397178	Mean dependent variable		0.447368
Durbin–Watson statistic	1.839673	Probability (*F*-statistic)		0.017439

Table 6.6 Morocco: data

Year	GDP/ head growth (% p.a.) (GHG)	Sec. Sch. enr't rate (%) (SSE)	Sec. Sch. enr't dummy (SCD)	Govt/ GDP (%) (GOP)	Inv./ GDP (%) (INP)	FDI/ Inv. (%) (FDP)	Economic reform dummy (REF)	FDI*SSE (F × S)
1973	1.5	14	0	7.5	18.1	−0.1	0	−1.5
1974	3.0	15	0	8.0	20.5	−1.3	0	−19.4
1975	4.2	16	0	10.5	31.9	0.0	0	−0.1
1976	8.7	17	0	13.6	33.7	1.2	0	20.6
1977	2.6	19	0	13.4	37.1	1.4	0	26.4
1978	0.6	20	0	13.9	26.7	1.3	0	26.8
1979	2.3	22	0	14.4	25.9	0.9	0	20.5
1980	6.8	26	0	12.7	24.9	1.9	0	49.7
1981	−5.2	26	0	13.7	25.6	1.5	0	38.9
1982	7.2	28	0	13.6	27.2	1.9	0	53.0
1983	−3.0	29	0	13.4	22.7	1.5	0	42.2
1984	1.8	33	0	13.5	13.5	2.7	0	89.5
1985	3.9	34	0	14.7	14.7	1.1	0	38.1
1986	5.6	36	0	15.4	15.4	0.0	1	0.7
1987	−4.5	37	0	15.7	15.7	2.0	1	74.8
1988	8.0	36	0	15.0	15.0	2.6	1	92.2
1989	0.1	36	0	14.6	14.6	5.0	1	180.5
1990	1.6	34	0	13.9	13.9	4.6	1	155.9
1991	3.7	28	0	13.7	13.7	8.4	1	236.1
1992	−6.1	28	0	15.4	15.4	9.7	1	271.8
1993	−3.3	28	0	16.6	16.6	11.1	1	311.5
Average	1.9	27		13.5	21.1	2.7		

Sources: World Bank, *World Tables* (various issues); IMF, *International Financial Statistics* (various issues).

Table 6.7 Morocco: growth, government size and skill levels

Dependent variable: GHG.
Method: least squares.
Sample(adjusted): 1975–1993.
Included observations: 19 after adjusting endpoints.

Variable	Coefficient	Standard error	*t*-statistic	Probability
C	13.22967	12.57960	1.051677	0.3086
GOP	−0.727384	0.928446	−0.783442	0.4448
F × S(−2)	−0.019238	0.018148	−1.060077	0.3049
R^2	0.186830	Mean dependent variable		1.842105
Durbin–Watson statistic	3.154351	Probability (*F*-statistic)		0.191184

Table 6.8 Tunisia: data

Year	GDP/ head growth (% p.a.) (GHG)	Sec. Sch. enr't rate (%) (SSE)	Sec. Sch. enr't dummy (SCD)	Govt/ GDP (%) (GOP)	Inv./ GDP (%) (INP)	FDI/ Inv. reform (%) (FDP)	Economic dummy (REF)	FDI × SSE (F × S)
1973	−2.1	19	0	16.4	35.2	6.915	0	131.4
1974	7.4	20	0	16.1	39.5	2.061	0	41.2
1975	5.3	21	0	16.8	36.3	3.237	0	68.0
1976	3.6	22	0	17.8	37.7	7.439	0	163.7
1977	−1.0	23	0	18.9	37.8	5.681	0	130.7
1978	4.1	24	0	18.4	39.2	4.451	0	106.8
1979	4.5	25	0	17.4	38.9	2.052	0	51.3
1980	5.9	27	0	17.6	36.2	8.566	0	231.3
1981	4.3	29	0	17.9	39.1	10.097	0	292.8
1982	−2.8	31	0	19.3	39.0	12.215	0	378.7
1983	2.4	33	0	19.5	36.4	4.376	0	144.4
1984	3.3	36	0	19.6	37.4	4.259	0	153.3
1985	3.2	39	0	19.3	31.0	4.542	0	177.1
1986	−3.9	39	0	19.8	25.6	3.122	0	121.8
1987	4.2	40	0	18.7	23.6	4.554	1	182.2
1988	−2.1	44	0	18.7	20.6	3.193	1	140.5
1989	−0.2	45	0	19.4	26.6	3.143	1	141.4
1990	5.1	45	0	18.6	29.5	2.360	1	106.2
1991	1.7	46	0	18.7	29.0	3.706	1	170.5
1992	5.5	43	0	18.1	32.0	8.326	1	358.0
1993	−0.5	43	0	18.3	31.6	5.917	1	254.4
Average	2.3	33		18.4	33.4	5.2		

Sources: World Bank, *World Tables* (various Issues); IMF, *International Financial Statistics* (various issues)

Table 6.9 Tunisia: growth, government size and skill levels

Dependent variable: GHG.
Method: least squares.
Sample (adjusted): 1975–1993.
Included observations: 19 after adjusting endpoints.

Variable	Coefficient	Standard error	*t*-statistic	Probability
C	55.89522	15.00119	3.726053	0.0018
GOP	−2.993463	0.847150	−3.533570	0.0028
F × S(−2)	0.012506	0.008707	1.436384	0.1702
R^2	0.449236	Mean dependent variable		2.242105
Durbin–Watson statistic	2.598621	Probability (*F*-statistic)		0.008467

References

Aghrout, A. (2000) *From Preferential Status to Partnership – The Euro-Maghreb Relationship*. Aldershot: Ashgate.

Algeria Agence Nationale de Développement de l'Investissement (2004). http://www.andi.gov.dz, accessed 12 May 2004.

Algeria (2001) Ordinance no. 1–03 of 20 August 2001 On the Development of Investments.

Algérie Presse Service (2004) 'IDE: 2,3 milliards USD dans le secteur des hydrocarbures en 2003'. http://www.aps.dz/fr/pageview.asp?ID = 60688, accessed 12 April 2004.

ANIMA (2002) Euro-Mediterranean Network of Investment Promotion Agencies. *Newsletter* no. 1, October 2002, p. 1.

ANIMA (2004a) Euro-Mediterranean Network of Investment Promotion Agencies. http://www.animaweb.org/index_en.php, accessed 17 May 2004.

ANIMA (2004b) 'Foreign Direct Investment in the MEDA Region in 2003', http://www.animaweb.org, accessed 04 April 2004.

Arabies (1995) no. 107, November 1995, p. 34.

Borensztein, E.R., J. De Gregorio and J.-W. Lee (1998) 'How Does Foreign Direct Investment Affect Economic Growth?', *Journal of International Economics*, 45, no., pp. 115–35.

Colton, N.A. (1999) 'The Maghrebi Economies as Emerging Markets', in Zoubir, Y.H., (ed.) *North Africa in Transition – State, Society and Economic Transformation*. Gainesville, FL: University Press of Florida.

El-Khabar (2004) Statement of the EU Delegates published in EI-Khabar (Algerian daily), 18 May 2004, p. 2–3.

Euro-Mediterranean (2004) Network of Investment Promotion Agencies. http://www.animaweb.org/index_en.php, accessed 17 May 2004.

European Commission (1995) *Barcelona Euro-Mediterranean Conference (27–28 November 1995) – Declaration and Work Programme,* DN: DOC/95/7, 4 December.

Eurostat (2003) *Statistics in Focus – Economy and Finance,* no. 13, p. 2.

Financial Times (1995) James Whillington 'Foreign Direct Investment: Agency Faces Formidable Task', *Financial Times* (Survey on Tunisia), 28 November 1995 p. IV.

Financial Times (1995) Roula Khalaf 'European Union Agreement. We have 12 years to adjust,' *Financial Times* (Survey on Morocco), 19 December 1995, p. 26.

IMF (monthly) *International Financial Statistics*. Washington, DC.

Mallampally, P. and K.P. Sauvant (1999) 'Foreign Direct Investment in Developing Countries', *Finance and Development,* 36, no. 1, pp.31–8.

Moran, T. (1998) *Foreign Direct Investment and Development: The New Policy Agenda for Developing Countries and Economies-in-Transition*. Washington, DC: Institute for International Economics.

Morocco (1995) Investment Charter, Law no. 18–95 of 8 November 1995 on the Investment Charter.

Morocco (2004) Ministère des Affaires Economiques/Direction des Investissements (Morocco), *Les Investissements Extérieurs au Maroc en 2003*, http://www.invest-in-morocco.gov.ma, accessed 15 May 2004.

Sonatrach (2002) http://www.sonatrach-dz.com, accessed 19 March 2002.

Tunisia (2004a) 'Invest in Tunisia', http://www.investintunisia.tn/ eng/poleA/pole0403.html, accessed 21 May 2004.

Tunisia (1994) 'Investment Incentives Code' in Tunisia. Law no. 93–120 of 27 December 1993 on Investment Incentives Code.

Tunisia (2004) Invest in Tunisia – FIPA, http://www.investintunisia.tn/eng/poleD/d0901.htm, accessed 19 May 2004.

UNCTAD (1998) *World Investment Report: Trends and Determinants*. New York: United Nations.

UNCTAD (2000) *Investment Regimes in the Arab World: Issues and Policies*. New York: United Nations.

UNCTAD (2002) *World Investment Report: Transnational Corporations and Export Competitiveness*. New York: United Nations.

UNCTAD (2003) *World Investment Report 2003 – FDI Policies for Development: National and International Perspectives*. New York: United Nations.

World Bank (2001) *World Development Indicators*. Washington, DC.

World Bank (2004) *Doing Business in 2004: Understanding Regulation*. Washington, DC: World Bank and Oxford University Press.

World Bank (various years) *World Tables*. Washington, DC.

7
The Impact of Foreign Direct Investment on Trade: Evidence from Tunisia's Trade

Rabiâa Mekki

Introduction

Over the last few years, some developing countries have built a strategy for economic development based on foreign investment in their economies. These countries have realized the key role of FDI in increasing industrialization and stimulating economic growth. The benefits of FDI appear technological transfer, employment, productivity gains, competitiveness and so on. In view of these considerations, attracting FDI has an integral element of policy reforms in many developing countries. Tunisia is no exception.

During the last decade, the Tunisian government was keen to encourage foreign investors to set up manufacturing plants in Tunisia by offering attractive investment incentives to export-oriented investments. Tunisia introduced an investment incentives code in 1994. It covers all the activity sectors with the exception of mining, energy, domestic trade and finance which are governed by specific texts. This code substantially improved and codified incentives for both national and foreign investors. The incentives can be either financial in the form of subsidies and grants, or fiscal in the form of waivers and tax reductions.

The Tunisian code of investment grants to all investors the tax incentives of 100 per cent for totally exporting activities, 50 per cent for investments environmental protection, development support activities and services, and 35 per cent for all activities covered by the investment code. These activities are eligible for suspension of value added tax (VAT) and consumption tax. Totally export companies have additional advantages. They benefit from total exemptions or reimbursements of customs duties and other taxes on imported capital equipment and production materials. In addition, these companies can put 20 per cent of their production on the local market. They have certain personal tax advantages, receive investment protection under treaty and are not subject to double taxation.

Additional incentives are available to promote investment in two free-trade zones in Tunisia, one in the north of the country at Bizerta and the other in the south at Zarzis. Companies which invest in these zones are exempt from most taxes and customs duties.

Tunisia has made considerable headway in attracting FDI. In addition to this legislation, bureaucratic formalities have been streamlined into one office: the '*guichet unique*'. Since 1999, the formalities for the constitution of companies may be carried out in this 'one-stop shop'. Starting in 1995, the Tunisian government set up a programme of privatization, which consisted largely of the sale of public enterprises. By the end of May 2002, 160 public enterprises were fully or partially privatized or were shut down and their assets sold off (UNCTAD 2003).[1]

To create and integrate markets and to enhance the credibility of domestic policies to foreign investors, Tunisia has entered into bilateral and regional trade agreements with the European Union (1995) and with the African, Arabic and Mediterranean nations.[2] During 1995–2002, Tunisia signed an important number of bilateral investment treaties (BITs).

The comparative advantages of Tunisia in terms of workforce, developed infrastructure, a geographical proximity to Europe and so on, in addition to its incentive policies have attracted important flows of foreign capitals. From 1990 to 2002, FDI in Tunisia increased by MTD[3] 77.5 to nearly MTD 1167.3 and non-energy investments moved up from MTD 24.5 to nearly MTD 739.8. On the other hand, 2503 foreign or joint-equity-owned companies operated in Tunisia with a stock of foreign investment of nearly TND18.1 billion by 2002. In the same period (1990 to 2002) exports went up from MTD 3087.4 to MTD 9749 and imports grew from MTD 4826.4 to MTD 13,510.9.[4]

During the 1990s, both FDI inflows into Tunisia and the international trade of Tunisia witnessed a tremendous increase. Is this a coincidence, or is there a special relationship between FDI and trade? Does FDI facilitate or restrict international trade? To what extent does FDI (affiliates' production and sales in a foreign market) replace or increase exports to the same market? What type of impact did FDI flows have on foreign trade: was it stimulated and if so, in what direction (imports or exports)? Who were the main investors and branches most attractive for investors?

The aim of this chapter is to investigate, through estimating an econometric model, the impact of FDI on trade. I seek to answer the questions: What is the role of FDI in Tunisia's trade; What is the impact of FDI on the structure of Tunisia's trade by sector? The chapter is structured as follows. In the second section I review the literature on the relationship between FDI and trade. In the third section I investigate empirically the impact of inward FDI on the structure of foreign trade by sector in Tunisia. The fourth section concludes the and contains the main findings.

Literature on FDI and trade

In this section, as a point of departure for exploring the impact of FDI on Tunisia's foreign trade, I begin with a brief survey of the theoretical and empirical literature on the FDI–trade relationship.

Theoretical studies

There has been, traditionally, a divergence in terms of the development of the theories dealing with FDI and international trade. Trade theory attempts to explain why countries trade with each other, FDI theory why firms produce abroad and invest in particular countries. In the neoclassical approach of trade theory, Mundell (1957) was the first to focus on the relationship between capital movements and the trade of commodities. In the Heckscher–Ohlin–Samuelson (HOS) framework, in taking account of the assumptions of perfect competition and constant economies of scale, Mundell argued that a tariff protection would generate a perfect substitution between capital movements and the trade of commodities.

Moreover, the question of complementarity/substitution was raised again with the new international theory developed at the end of the 1970s and dealing with imperfect competition and increasing economies of scale.

In the beginning, Vernon (1966) developed the famous product cycle model, stating that FDI affiliates' production and sales in a foreign market replace trade in the same market. Moreover, the 'electric theory' or the ownership, location and internalization (OLI) paradigm developed by Dunning (1981) points out that trade and FDI are alternative strategies for multinational firms. In general, such a microeconomic analysis of firms' internalization choices predicts this substitute relationship between FDI and trade.

Some earlier theoretical work has predicted either a substitute or a complementary relationship between FDI and trade. These models are based on the imperfect competition, the economies of scale, the difference in production technologies and so on. Some have focused mainly on either vertical or horizontal FDI. In the first case, a firm separates geographically the different stages in its value-added chain. In the second case, it duplicates the entire production process in several countries with the exception of headquarters activities.

The models of Helpman (1984) and Helpman and Krugman (1985) integrate vertical FDI into international trade theory. They show that FDI generates complementary trade flows of finished goods from foreign affiliates to parent companies or to the home country and intra-firm transfers of intangible headquarters services from parent companies to foreign affiliates.

On the other hand, in the models based on horizontal FDI, such as Markusen (1983), Brainard (1993), Horstmann and Markusen (1992), Markusen and Venables (1995) and Markusen (1995), trade and foreign investment are alternative modalities. The choice a multinational firm makes depends on the interaction between the following key elements: firm-specific advantages (activities of research and development, managerial know-how and so on), plant-level economies of scale, and transport costs (geographical and cultural distance costs). In these models, the substitutability between FDI and trade prevails over complementarity.

According to the models of Brainard (1993) and Horstmann and Markusen (1992), when countries are identical in technologies, preferences and factor endowments, the higher the value of firm-level economies of scale and tariffs and transport costs relative to plant-level economies of scale, the more likely is the presence of horizontal FDI. These models based on the trade-off between proximity and concentration postulate a substitution relationship between horizontal FDI and trade.

Markusen and Venables (1995) further elaborated the theory to introduce asymmetries between countries in terms of market size, factor endowments, and technologies. Countries' asymmetries make it possible for national and multinational firms, and therefore trade and FDI, to coexist. However, as countries become more similar in market size, relative factor endowments, and technical efficiency, FDI will increase and international economic activity will become increasingly dominated by MNEs, which displace trade, provided transport costs are not very small.

The contributions within the theoretical literature show the ambiguity of the relationship between FDI and international trade. The conclusions of models are shared between substitutability and complementarity.

Empirical studies

Empirical studies of the relationship between FDI and trade can be classified as either macroeconomic or microeconomic.

Macroeconomic studies use macroeconomic data series of FDI and trade. In this context, the model of Eaton and Tamura (1994) analyses the American and Japanese bilateral flows of both FDI and trade with a great number of partners for the period 1985–90 and uses a modified gravitational model with factor endowments. The authors argue that the correlation between outflows investment and exports and the correlation between inflows investment and imports are positive: FDI seems to improve trade. They conclude that FDI induces trade and vice versa (the complementarity relationship).

However, Eaton and Tamura (1994) do not consider the sectoral aspect of trade and FDI, which represents a limitation to their model. Fontagné and Pajot (1997) try to remedy these limitations and propose a bilateral and sectoral empirical approach of the relationship between FDI and trade. Their estimations are based on data of different and coherent levels of disaggregation for France, Italy, Japan, Netherlands, Sweden, EU, and the USA (12) for the period 1984–94. First, for a panel of 19 French industries the authors found that FDI flows and French foreign trade are mutually complementary. Outward FDI is associated with additional exports and imports (a trade surplus). Inversely, inward FDI is associated with a trade deficit of the host country. At the macroeconomic level, the authors concluded, a large share of the complementarity between trade and FDI can be accounted for by the spillovers between industries.

Some other studies, like the CEPII[5] (1998) report and Fontagné *et al.* (1998) confirm the complementarity between trade and FDI. For EU members, Fontagné *et al.* (1998) note that the complementarity is more pronounced in the intra-industries trade than in the inter-industries one.

At the microeconomic level, studies use either individual or aggregated data of multinational activities. The studies of Lipsey and Weiss (1981, 1984) are famous in this domain. In their paper (1984) related to the American case, Lipsey and Weiss use disaggregating data by industry, location of investment and destination of exports, and make a distinction between finished products and intermediate goods. Lipsey and Weiss confirm that the foreign production of the American firms does not substitute for exports of the host country. Also in this study the complementarity hypothesis is validated.

The empirical relationship between FDI and trade: sectoral analysis

This section analyses the empirical relationship between trade flows and Tunisian FDI inflows. On one hand, I estimate the relationship between Tunisian exports and FDI inflows. On the other hand, I estimate the relationship between Tunisian imports and FDI inflows. I use a panel of data set at sectoral level for Tunisian manufacturing industries in the period 1990–2003. The data available for both FDI and trade are related to six manufacturing industries:

1. miscellaneous manufacturing industries;
2. agro-food industries;
3. building materials;
4. mechanical and electrical industries;
5. chemical industries;
6. textile–clothing and leather–footwear.

Standard specification and variables definition

The standard model can be specified in equations (7.1) and (7.2). In equation (7.1), I estimate the impact of FDI inflows on Tunisian exports in the case of manufacturing industries:

$$\ln Xport_{it} = \alpha + \beta_1 \ln FDI_{it} + \beta_2 \ln GDPW_t + \beta_3 \ln REER + u_{it} \quad (7.1)$$

Where $i = 1, \ldots, 6$, $t = 1990, \ldots, 2003$, and u_{it} refers to the disturbance term for the industry i at time (year) t. The dependent variable is $Xport_{it}$: exports of Tunisia by industry i at time t. The independent variables are FDI_{it}: foreign direct investment inflows by industry i at time t; $GDPW_t$: gross domestic product of the world in real terms at time t; *REER*: effective exchange rate of the Tunisian dinar.

In equation (7.2), I estimate the impact of FDI inflows on Tunisian imports in the case of manufacturing industries:

$$\ln Mport_{it} = \alpha + \beta_1 \ln FDI_{it} + \beta_2 \ln GDPT + \beta_3 \ln REER + u_{it} \quad (7.2)$$

Where $i = 1, \ldots, 6$, $t = 1990, \ldots, 2003$. The dependent variable is $Mport_{it}$: imports of Tunisia by industry i at time t. The independent variables are FDI_{it}: foreign direct investment inflows by industry i at time t; $GDPT_{it}$ gross domestic product of Tunisia in real terms at time t; *REER*: effective exchange rate of the Tunisian dinar.

The data on FDI are obtained from FIPA (foreign investment promotion agency). Data on exports, imports and the GDP of Tunisia are obtained from the NIS (National Institute of Statistics). Finally, the data on the GDP of the world and REER are extracted from the CEPII database: CHELEM (Comptes Harmonisés sur les Echanges et l'Economie Mondiale).

Results of estimations

To investigate the relationship between FDI and trade, I use three econometric models: fixed-effects, random-effects and least-squares. The results are grouped in Table 7.1 for exports and in Table 7.2 for imports. In addition I present the coefficients of determination adjusted ($\overline{R^2}$)and a diagnostic test: *H* is Hausman's test on the correlation between the individual effects and the explanatory variables (that is a test of the fixed-effects model against the random-effects model), distributed as a chi-squared. In both the estimation of exports and imports equations (see Tables 7.1 and 7.2), the Hausman test shows that the fixed-effects model is preferred to the random-effects model.

The estimations results of equation (7.1) are presented in Table 7.1. A first result concerns the coefficient of FDI inflows, which is positive but weak (0.002). The FDI stimulates the export of manufacturing industries in Tunisia. In addition, I found that the coefficients of GDPW are consistently positive and statistically significant in all

Table 7.1 Estimation of exports equation (7.1) for a panel of six manufacturing industries, Tunisia 1990–2003

	Fixed-effects model	**Random-effects model**	**OLS model**
Constant		−3.082[a]	0.377
		(−0.98)	(0.031)
FDI	0.002	0.002	0.165[a]
	(0.109)	(0.111)	(2.781)
GDPW	3.341[a]	3.325[a]	3.238[a]
	(10.89)	(11.921)	(10.462)
REER	−1.473	−1.473	3.828
	(−0.519)	(−0.527)	(0.344)
$\overline{R^2}$	0.94	0.94	0.07
Hausman test	32.51[a]		

[a] denotes significance at the levels of 1%.

Table 7.2 Estimation of imports equation (7.2) for a panel of six manufacturing industries, Tunisia 1990–2003

	Fixed-effects model	**Random-effects model**	**OLS model**
Constant		−4.411[a]	−1.949
		(−1.957)	(−0.156)
FDI	0.033[a]	0.033[a]	0.14[a]
	(2.15)	(2.186)	(2.242)
GDPT	1.018[a]	1.018[a]	0.965
	(3.502)	(3.561)	(0.512
REER	0.805	0.707	1.567
	(0.539)	(1.117)	(0.211)
$\overline{R^2}$	0.97	0.97	0.06
Hausman test	86.01[a]		

[a] denotes significance at the level of 1%.

regressions (3.341). The GDP of the world is expected to have a positive effect on Tunisian exports. Another important finding concerns the coefficient of REER, which is negative and not significant in the exports equation (−1.473). Such a result can be explained by the policy of the rate exchange stabilization in Tunisia since the 1990s.

The estimations results of equation (7.2) are presented in Table 7.2. First, the coefficient of FDI inflows is positive and significant (0.033).

Table 7.3 Estimation of individual effect by industries, Tunisia 1990–2003

	Exports	Imports
Textiles and Leather	2.243[a]	2.18
	(1.384)	(1.213)
Agro-food industries	0.741	1.506
	(0.458)	(0.838)
Building materials	−0.1014	−0.986
	(−0.626)	(−0.548)
Mechanical and Electrical industries	1.006	2.684[b]
	(0.621)	(1.493)
Chemical industries	0.948	1.427
	(0.585)	(0.794)
Miscellaneous manufacturing industries	−0.84	0.666
	(−0.518)	(0.37)
$\overline{R^2}$	0.97	0.97

[a] and [b] denote significance at the level of 1% and 15% respectively.

The FDI stimulates the imports of the Tunisian manufacturing industries. This result seems to reinforce the hypothesis of complementarity between FDI and trade. Second, I found that the coefficients of GDPT were consistently positive and statistically significant (1.018). The GDP of the Tunisia captures the size of Tunisia's internal market. A higher GDP is assumed to imply an important demand. Consequently, I consider the GDP of Tunisia as an indicator of its foreign demand and determine its imports. Finally, in the imports equation the coefficient of REER is positive and not significant (0.805). This result shows that the exchange rate has a positive impact on the Tunisian imports.

In a second stage, I estimate the individual effect of FDI by industries for the same period (1990–2003). The estimations results are presented in Table 7.3.

I can summarize the principal results obtained for manufacturing industries considered individually, in the following three points:

1. FDI in Tunisian manufacturing industries is associated with additional exports and imports in four sub-industries.
   - *Textile and leather*: US$1 FDI in this industry is associated with US$2.2 of exports and with US$2.1 of imports. In reference to

the report of the Tunisian central bank, about 68 per cent of exports and 66 per cent of imports under the offshore regime were in the textiles and leather sector, which has a large number of non-resident firms. Textile and leather industries for a long time constituted one of the most dynamic sectors at the level of exports. Advantages granted by the EU within the framework of Arrangement have certainly boosted this sector, but they established a major obstacle for the emergence of industries with strong added value.

- *Mechanical and electrical industries*: US$1 FDI in mechanical and electrical industries is associated with US$1 of exports and with US$2.7 of imports. This result can be explained by the considerable growth of FDI in this industry. In the last years, mechanical and electrical industries attracted more FDI, which grew from MDT 3.17 in 1990 to MDT 35.77 in 2000. The imports for 1995–2000 doubled, rising from MDT 2612.0 in 1995 to MDT 4774 in 2000.
- *Chemical industries*: US$1m. FDI in chemical industries increases both the imports and the exports, by US$1.4m. and US$0.9m. respectively. The impact of FDI on imports is stronger than on exports.
- *Agro food industries*: US$1m. FDI in agro-food industries is associated with US$0.7m of exports and with US$1.5m. of imports.

2. FDI replaces exports in two industries: miscellaneous manufacturing industries in which US$1 FDI decreases the exports by US$0.8m. and building materials in which US$1 FDI decreases the exports by US$0.1.
3. FDI replaces imports in one industry: building materials, in which US$1 FDI decreases the imports by US$1.

The Tunisian manufacturing industries are dominated by SMEs (small and medium enterprises) and by affiliates of MNEs which take advantage of the low costs of production in Tunisia. These affiliates import intermediate goods from the parent companies and export finished goods to parent companies. Despite the heterogeneity of the results obtained at the industrial level, the complementarity between FDI and both exports and imports of Tunisian manufacturing industries is confirmed.

Conclusion

This chapter has investigated the relationship between FDI and trade. The theoretical models show the ambiguity of the relationship between FDI and international trade. Some earlier theoretical models have focused mainly on either vertical or horizontal FDI, and have predicted either a substitute relationship between FDI and trade or a complementary one. Yet some empirical studies, using either macroeconomic or microeconomic data series, have revealed a positive relationship between FDI and trade.

In my empirical study, I chose to test if FDI in the Tunisian manufacturing industries is associated with additional exports and imports for these industries. To examine this relationship, I used a panel-data econometric methodology. Data available for both FDI and trade are related to six manufacturing industries in the period 1990–2003. My basic conclusions are summarized in the following points.

First, the key finding of this study is that FDI has a positive impact on promoting Tunisian manufacturing trade flows with the rest of the world. Therefore, the regression results are consistent with a complementarity relationship between FDI and both exports and imports. FDI inflows are associated with additional exports and imports.

Second, I notice that at industry level the nature of the relationship between FDI and trade (complementarity or substitution) varies for each industry and depends on its characteristics. My results from estimating the effect for individual industries show that FDI in Tunisian manufacturing industries is associated with additional exports and imports in textile and leather, mechanical and electrical, chemical and agro-food industries. However, FDI replaces trade flows in building materials and miscellaneous manufacturing industries. At the industry level, I underline the strong sectoral specificity of the relationship between FDI and trade.

Finally, my model has some limitations because the period of estimation is quite short. This is because the data on FDI into individual manufacturing industries are not available.

Notes

1. UNCTAD: United Nations Conference on Trade and Development.

2. Tunisia signed free-trade agreements with Egypt, Morocco, Jordan and Libya in 2001.
3. MTD: million Tunisian dinars (TND1 = US$0.704 = €0.745 = JP¥ 88.492).
4. National Institute of Statistics (NIS).
5. CEPII: Centre d'Etudes Prospectives et d'Information Internationales.

References

Brainard, S.L. (1993) *A Simple Theory of Multinational Corporations and Trade with a Trade-off Between Proximity and Concentration*, NBER Working Paper no. 4269, February 1993.

CEPII (1998) 'Commerce international et investissement direct: amis ou ennemis?' in *Compétitivité des Nations*, Paris: Economica, 183–200.

Dunning, J.H. (1981) *International Production and the Multinational Enterprise*, London: Allen Unwin.

Eaton, J. and A. Tamura (1994) 'Bilateralism and Regionalism in Japanese and U.S. Trade and Direct Foreign Investment Patterns', *Journal of Japanese and International Economics*, 8(4), 478–510.

Fontagné, L., Freudenberg M. and N. Péridy (1998) 'Commerce international et structures de marché: Une vérification empirique', *Economie et Prévision*, no. 135(1998–4), 147–67.

Fontagné, L. and M. Pajot (1997) *How Foreign Direct Investment Affects International Trade and Competitiveness: an Empirical Assessment*. CEPII, document de travail no. 97-17, December.

Helpman, E. (1984) 'A Simple Theory of International Trade with Multinational Corporations', *Journal of Political Economy*, 92(3), 451–71.

Helpman, E. and P.R. Krugman (1985) *Market Structure and Foreign Trade*. Cambridge, MA and London: MIT Press.

Horstmann, I.J. and J.R. Markusen (1992) 'Endogenous Market Structures in International Trade', *Journal of International Economics*, 32(1–2), 109–29.

Lipsey, R.E. and M.Y. Weiss (1981) 'Foreign Production and Exports in Manufacturing Industries', *Review of Economics and Statistics*, 63 (4), 488–94.

Lipsey, R.E. and M.Y. Weiss (1984) 'Foreign Production and Exports of Individual firms', *Review of Economics and Statistics*, 66(2), 304–8.

Markusen, J.R. (1983) 'Factor Movements and Commodity Trade as Complements', *Journal of International Economics*, 14(3–4), 341–56.

Markusen, J.R. (1995) 'The Boundaries of Multinational Enterprises and the Theory of International Trade', *Journal of Economic Perspectives*, 9(2), 169–89.

Markusen, J.R. and Venables (1995) *Multinational Firms and the New Trade Theory*, NBER Working paper no. 5036.

Mundell, R.A. (1957) 'International Trade and Factor Mobility', *American Economic Review*, 47(3), 321–35.

UNCTAD (2003) *World Investment Report*, New York, United Nations.

Vernon R. (1966) 'International Investment and International Trade in the Product Life Cycle', *Quarterly Journal of Economics*, 80(2), 190–207.

8

Foreign Direct Investment Inflows into Emerging Markets: Driving Forces and Lessons for Africa

Honest Prosper Ngowi

Introduction

Foreign direct investment (FDI) has been referred to as an engine of growth, especially in a developing country. This is based on the fact that it can potentially play a vital role in the process of economic development. FDI for example is known to create new jobs and retain old ones, provide needed capital investment, contribute to government coffers, and bring new, advanced and state-of-the art technologies among other advantages. No wonder then that countries are actively bidding to attract more FDI inflows. Despite the fact that virtually all countries are making efforts to attract more FDI inflows, the global distribution of these investments is highly skewed. The lion's share has traditionally been flowing into the Triad (the USA, Japan and the European Union – EU). In the recent past, it has been observed however that a substantial amount of FDI is starting to flow into the emerging markets, especially those in Asia, Central and Eastern Europe. Africa, on the contrary, has been lagging behind in attracting these essential investments for its development in general and poverty reduction in particular. This chapter attempts to describe the driving forces behind FDI inflows into the emerging markets of Asia, Central and Eastern Europe. It further attempts to identify some lessons that Africa can learn from these markets in its bid to attract more FDI.

On FDI

A foreign direct investment is one made to acquire a lasting interest in a foreign enterprise with the purpose of having an effective voice in its management. It is an investment in the business of another country, which often takes the form of setting up local production facilities or the purchase of existing business (Rutherford 1995:178–9).

FDIs are normally undertaken by multinational companies in different countries. They may take the form of new or greenfield investments. Alternatively they may be acquisitions of existing projects through mergers and acquisitions (M&A).

Among the conditions that motivate firms to choose FDI as a mode of entry to foreign markets are those employed in Dunning's OLI theory: firms are likely to prefer FDI to other entry modes[1] if they have ownership advantages (O), location advantages (L) and internalization advantages (I) (for details see Dunning 1992).

FDI determinants

FDI determinants are the factors that determine FDI inflows into a given geographical location, say a country or a region. They give investors the confidence needed to invest in foreign markets. It should be mentioned that the list of these determinants can be very long. But not all determinants are equally important to every investor in every location all the time. In a given location at a given time, some determinants may be more important to one investor than to another. A given determinant may be a necessary and satisfactory factor by itself for FDI inflow in one location but not in another. Some determinants may be closely related to each other. Most of them are complementary to one another rather than being mutually exclusive.

UNCTAD's 1998 World Investment Report presents some host country determinants of FDI. These include the following.

Policy framework for FDI: economic, political and social stability; rules regulating entry and operations (of FDIs); standard of treatment of foreign affiliates; policies on functioning and structure of the markets; International agreement on FDI; privatization policy; trade policy (tariffs and non-tariff barriers and coherence of FDI and trade policy); tax policy.

Economic determinants: business facilitation including: investment promotion through image-building and investment-generating activities and investment facilitating services; investment incentives; hassle costs (related to corruption and administrative efficiency); social amenities (for example bilingual schools, quality of life; after-investment services.

UNCTAD (1998) matches types of FDIs by motives of the firms with some principal economic determinants. Below is the matching.

Market-seeking FDI looks for: market size and per capita income; market growth; access to regional and global markets; country-specific consumer preferences; structure of markets.

Resource/asset-seeking FDI looks for: raw materials; low-cost unskilled labour; skilled labour; technological, innovative and other created assets (like brand names) including as embodied in individuals, firms and clusters; physical infrastructure (ports, roads, power, telecommunications).

Efficiency-seeking FDI looks for: costs of resources and assets listed above, adjusted for labour productivity; other input costs, such as transport and communications costs to/from and within host economy and other intermediate products; membership of a regional integration agreement conducive to the establishment of regional corporate networks.

On multinational companies

The literature provides several definitions of a multinational enterprise (MNE). Some refer to it a transnational corporations (TNCs), a multinational corporations (MNC), a multinational company or simply a Multinational. Here these may all be used interchangeably to mean one and the same thing unless otherwise stated. It is the author's view that the concept of FDI is inseparable from the concept of the multinational because it is multinationals that undertake FDI.

In a rather long and elaborative definition, Donald Rutherford (1995:311), drawing from Caves's (1982) work on multinational enterprises and economic analysis, defines an MNC as: 'an international firm that produces goods or services in several countries, without being concentrated in a single country'. Although the term became popular in the 1960s, by the late nineteenth century several US, British and Dutch firms had acquired such characteristics.

The advantages of production abroad, rather than export from the country of original operation, include a saving in transport costs, the adjustment of the product design to make it more acceptable to local markets, a reduction, in many cases, in corporate taxation, and access to local labour and capital which may be more abundant than at home. The immense success of this organizational form, prominent in many industries, including motor cars, computers, pharmaceuticals, food-processing, oil and soap, has attracted both envy and criticism: envy from national governments with less economic power and competence, criticism from Marxists who see the growth of multinationals as a sinister international expansion of capitalism. Also, trade unions complain about competition from cheap-labour countries; science graduates lament the increased concentration of R&D activities in the USA to the detriment of other countries; national governments object to the loss of tax revenue and the difficulties of operating industrial and employment policies when much of their industrial sector is controlled by foreign-owned entities.

Many controls have been suggested in order to reduce what is seen to be the less attractive effects of multinationals: governments and trade unions lay down strict conditions for foreign countries wishing to invest, fiscal devices are used to maintain tax revenues and domestically owned multinationals are monitored. In extreme cases exasperated national governments have nationalized the assets of foreign-owned subsidiaries: but in many cases this has been as sensible as cutting the hands off a worker and expecting the severed hands to do the same work as before – a subsidiary unsupported by the services of the rest of the corporation is a poor shadow of its former self. Despite so many attempts to curb the activities of multinationals, they continue to grow, enjoying all the benefits of economies of scale and retaining their status as major world economic institutions.

FDI inflows into the emerging markets

According to UNCTAD (2004) the emerging markets, especially in Asia, Central and Eastern Europe, are likely to be FDI hotspots in the period 2004–7. Of the expected 11 global FDI hotspots, 9 (82 per cent) are in the emerging markets of Asia, Latin America and Central and Eastern Europe. Out of these 9, only 1 (11 per cent) is in Latin America.

6 of the 9 (67 per cent) are in Asia. 2 of the 9 (22 per cent) are in Central and Eastern Europe.

More specifically, China and India are the leading hotspots for FDI, followed by the USA, Thailand, Poland, the Czech Republic, Mexico, Malaysia, the UK, Singapore and the Republic of Korea.

In Asia and the Pacific, optimism about FDI prospects is broad-based in terms of industries. There are prospects for both manufacturing and service sectors. Contrary to the global trend, the emerging markets of Latin America are expected to attract more natural-resource-based FDI. In Central and Eastern Europe there are prospects in the increased flow in both the manufacturing and service sectors. According to UNCTAD (2004:2) there is less optimism about prospects in the short term for Africa than for other parts of the world.

Driving forces behind FDI inflows into the emerging markets

Driving forces behind FDI inflows into a given location can be looked at from different perspectives. Among the perspectives are looking at the entry modes and then looking at the driving forces behind a specific entry mode. Another perspective is by looking at the efforts done by FDI destinations (countries) to attract more of these investments. A third way to determine the driving forces could be to get the views of the MNE or MNEs on the specific driving forces behind their presence in a specific FDI destination. The first two perspectives will be used in this work. The third would involve field-visiting for data collection. Being short of resources to do the field visit, the author proposes this as among the possible areas of future research.

Efforts by countries to attract FDI as a driving force

It is an undisputed fact that countries active in trying to attract more FDI are more likely to convince MNEs to locate their FDI projects in them than are dormant ones. Among the ways countries can convince MNEs to locate their FDI projects in them include policy measures. In the case of the emerging markets of Asia and Central and Eastern Europe several policy measures were used to influence FDI inflows in 2003, among them additional incentives, further liberalization and greater targeting.

Incentives

There is a wide spectrum of FDI incentives. These include tax incentives, guarantees against arbitrary treatment in the case of nationalization, government provision of such utilities as water, power and communication at subsidized prices or free of cost, tariffs or quotas set for competing imports, the reduction or elimination of import duties on inputs, interest rate subsidies, the guarantee of loans and coverage for exchange rate risks, wage subsidies, training grants and the relaxation of legal obligations towards employees.

Liberalization

Economic liberalization is among the policy measures a country can take to attract more FDI. The areas where most countries have liberalized include trade (internal and external trade), exchange rates, prices and interest rates. Countries that have liberalized these activities have principally left the free interplay of market forces of supply and demand at work, with minimal government intervention where necessary.

Targeting

In targeting, countries focus on the types of investment they need and then solicit investors that can bring them. They seek not just to attract investors at large, but rather strive to attract those willing to invest in specific sectors, for example electronics. Table 8.1 presents some policy measures taken by the emerging markets of Asia and

Table 8.1 Policy measures taken by the emerging markets to attract FDIs in 2003

The figures are in percentages, indicating the percentage of the 87 international location experts asked in UNCTAD (2004) to give their opinions on FDI prospects, *inter alia*, for the period 2004–7.

Policy measure	**Asia**	**Central and Eastern Europe**
No new measure	21	25
Additional incentives	43	59
Further liberalization	65	59
Greater targeting	33	42
Others	17	9

Source: Adapted by the author from UNCTAD (2004).

Table 8.2 Policy measures to be taken by the emerging markets to attract FDIs in 2004–5

The figures are in percentages, indicating the percentage of the 87 international location experts surveyed in UNCTAD (2004) to give their opinions on FDI prospects, *inter alia*, for the period 2004–7.

Policy measure	**Asia**	**Central and Eastern Europe**
No new measure	19	15
Additional incentives	51	39
Further liberalization	81	83
Greater targeting	48	61
Others	13	22

Source: Adapted by the author from UNCTAD (2004).

Central and Eastern Europe to attract more FDI inflows in 2003. The driving forces (policy measures) behind FDI inflows into the emerging markets for the period 2004–5, according to UNCTAD (2004) are expected to be as presented in Table 8.2.

From Tables 8.1 and 8.2 it can be generally seen that, among other things, further liberalization of the emerging markets economics of Asia and Central and Eastern Europe is considered to be the major driving force for FDI inflows there. This policy measure is followed by provision of additional investment incentives to investors in these markets, especially in Asia. The third policy measure in the two emerging markets is greater targeting, especially in Central and Eastern Europe.

Entry modes as a driving force

MNEs engaging in FDIs have different entry modes to host countries. They may do so through the expansion of existing enterprise by acquiring or merging with existing local firms in the form of mergers and acquisitions (M&As). They may also enter a country through investments in new enterprises in the form of greenfield investments. In addition to these two FDI entry modes is brownfield investment, a hybrid situation between greenfield and acquisition. Each type of entry mode will now be briefly described.

Mergers and acquisitions (M&As)

M&As involve expansion of existing firms through joint ventures (mergers) between firms and acquisitions through one firm purchasing another. M&As can be cross-border or domestic in nature. This work deals with cross-border M&As as they are the ones relevant in the context of FDI. Therefore, unless otherwise specified M&As in this work will be used to mean cross-border M&As. Functionally we can differentiate between horizontal M&As (between competing firms in the same industry), vertical M&As (between firms in client–supplier or buyer–seller relationships and conglomerates (between companies in unrelated industries). See UNCTAD (2000) for details.

According to UNCTAD (2000:10), most of the growth in international production over the last decade has been via M&As (defined as the acquisition of more than a 10 per cent equity share) rather than greenfield investment.

Greenfield investments

A firm making a greenfield investment in a foreign market has to establish new production facilities there from scratch, as opposed to obtaining existing ones via M&A. Greenfield investment therefore gives the investing firm a higher degree of flexibility, while ownership advantages are easier to transfer to a new venture. The greater technological and organizational flexibility of this entry mode may also translate into lower production costs. A firm may also favour greenfield investment over M&A when the internalization of knowledge is important to it. This is because the possibility of controlling the use of such knowledge may be weaker in the case of M&A.

Greenfield investment is likely to be relatively more important for a firm with a technological edge over its competitors. The first reason for this is that a firm possessing strong technological advantage over its competitor may not be too worried about competition. It is therefore less inclined to choose acquisition in order to reduce the competitive pressure in the market. Second, a highly efficient firm would tend to choose greenfield investment in order to implement its technology in an efficient manner. Third, greenfield investment may be chosen in order to protect a firm's technology.

Greenfield investment is a form of organic growth. This entry mode may be preferred to M&A, which is a form of external growth, because it gives firms greater flexibility in choosing appropriate locations. It enables them to build scales of plants most appropriate to their operations, and to install modern manufacturing processes, techniques and work practices. Firms are therefore likely to avoid such problems as those associated with the rationalization and reorganization of existing plants and the removal of restrictive labour practices.

Brownfield investments

Brownfield investment is a hybrid between greenfield investment and acquisition. In this case, investments that are formally an acquisition resemble greenfield projects. A foreign investor acquires a firm in this case, but almost completely replaces plant and equipment, labour and product lines (see Meyer and Saul: 1998 for details). The concept of brownfield investments has been applied mostly in cases of acquisitions in transition economies.

Driving forces behind entry modes

M&As

This section borrows much from UNCTAD (2000). Speed and access to proprietary assets are identified by UNCTAD (2000:140) as the two major driving forces behind M&As.

M&As represent the fastest means for FDI to enter a market when speed is crucial. For example, when time to market is vital, the takeover of an existing firm in a new market with an established distribution system is by far preferable to developing a new local distribution and marketing organization. M&As can provide a way for a late comer to catch up rapidly in a market or a new field of technology.

The quest for strategic assets is the second major driving force behind M&As. Such assets include R&D or technical know-how, patents, brand names, the possession of local permits and licences, and supplier or distribution networks. Ready-made access to proprietary assets can be important because they are not available elsewhere in the market and they take time to develop.

These two major driving forces interact with a number of others, which play out differently in different industries and markets. These other driving forces may also motivate FDI in general, but when speed enters the picture they tend to favour M&As, as the objectives sought for can be realized more quickly. The other driving forces are explained in what follows.

The search for new markets and market power may drive firms to enter a market through M&As. This entry mode enables firms to quickly access new market opportunities and develop critical mass without adding additional capacity to an industry. M&As enable immediate access to a local network of suppliers, clients and skills. The access is important because the need for knowledge about local conditions is important when entering new foreign markets.

Firms may also choose M&As owing to anticipated gains in efficiency through synergies. Synergies can be static or dynamic. While the former involves cost reduction or revenue enhancement at a given point in time, the latter involves innovation enhancing. Static synergies may include the pooling of management resources, revenue enhancement by using each other's marketing and distribution networks, purchasing synergies, economies of scale and avoidance of duplication of production, R&D or other activities. Dynamic synergies may involve the matching of complementary resources and skills to enhance a firm's innovatory capabilities.

Greater size is another driving force behind M&As. This can be a crucial parameter in a globalizing economy, especially when economies of scale, a large expenditure on R&D and the expansion of distribution networks are required. Size can create financial, operational and managerial synergies that reduce the operational vulnerability of firms. Large firms, with multiple operations across geographical locations and segments, can have an advantage in the location and adoption of new information and innovation.

Another driver behind M&As is the desire for risk reduction through product or geographical market diversification. Firms may choose M&As on the basis that industry returns across countries may be less correlated than within an economy. M&As may also enable firms to circumvent tariff and non-tariff barriers (NTBs).

M&As may be driven by personal gains. According to Baumol (1967), corporate managers may pursue their own self-interest to enhance executive power, prestige, job security or remuneration, even when this is not technically efficient or in the interest of shareholders. They can also be under pressure by financial markets to show high growth and profit rates. Here M&As can provide an easier route to high growth than organic greenfield investment.

Other driving forces behind M&As include the rapid pace of technological change, which has intensified competitive pressures. Firms now need to make more effort to maintain innovative leads, to find new areas of technological leadership, and to keep up with new knowledge and shorter product life-cycles. M&As allow firms to do all of these things more quickly.

Changes in the policy and regulatory environment in the past decade or so are another M&As driver. The changes include the liberalization of FDI and trade regimes – including more efforts to attract FDI by several countries, the removal of restrictions, active promotion, and the provision of high standards of treatment, legal protection and guarantees.

Regional free-trade areas enlarge the size of the immediately accessible market for firms, and therefore attract FDI. Trade liberalization makes firms face more intense competition at home as well as abroad. Widespread privatization and deregulation have provided another stimulus for M&As. Privatization in developing countries and economies in transition have increased the availability of domestic companies for sale.

Another driver is the changes in the capital markets. Liberalization of capital movements, new information technology providing instant information across the globe, more active market intermediaries and new financial instruments have had a profound impact on M&A activities worldwide. A supply of suitable target firms to acquire in host economies is also a driving force behind M&As.

UNCTAD (2000:145) mentions that the advantages of M&As in developing countries rarely include access to proprietary technology or skills. They are, rather, rapid market entry, local market knowledge, established distribution systems and contacts with the government, suppliers or customers.

There are some firm-specific characteristics that seem to favour M&As over greenfield FDIs. These include lower R&D intensity, highly diversified investments, large MNEs, lower cultural and economic distance between home and host countries, MNEs that already have an affiliate in a host country and slow growth in an industry (see UNCTAD 2000:145 for details).

It should be mentioned that seldom is only one factor decisive when firms choose entry modes.

Greenfield investments

This sub section presents some general driving forces behind greenfield investments. When a host country has investment opportunities but there are few firms to acquire, an MNE has to enter through greenfield investment. This is the case in most developing countries with a relatively poorly developed industrial sector and capital markets.

FDI policy in host economies may oblige entry through greenfield investments. The liberalization of FDI regimes in most cases applies for both M&As and greenfield investments. But in some countries foreign takeovers are *de facto* (if not *de jure*) restricted. The restriction can be a general one or apply to a particular industry. In such cases multinationals may be forced to enter through greenfield investments.

Some institutional framework may also be a driving force behind greenfield investments. For example differences in corporate governance and ownership structure between countries may influence MNEs to choose greenfield investments. Underdeveloped asset markets and poor accounting standards in developing countries may make it more difficult to assess accurately the value of corporate assets and therefore lead to greenfield investments instead of M&As.

Some firm-specific characteristics have been identified in UNCTAD (2000:145) as possible driving forces behind greenfield investments. These are given below.

Firms with stronger technological advantages tend to prefer greenfield investments to a greater extent than do those without. Less-diversified investing firms are likely to choose greenfield investments than are more-diversified ones.

Smaller firms are traditionally more prone to enter through greenfield investment than are larger ones. The greater the cultural and economic distance between home and host countries, the greater is the probability of greenfield investment. Large asset prises and perfections in capital markets would encourage more greenfield investments than M&As.

Rapid growth in an industry may favour greenfield investments. Industries characterized by undercapacity, rising prises and rapid growth are likely to attract more greenfield FDIs than M&As.

FDI entry modes and their driving forces have been dicussed above. In Table 8.3, the expected FDI entry modes into the emerging markets of Asia and Central and Eastern Europe are presented. The table suggests that the leading entry mode for Asia and Central and Eastern European emerging markets is most likely to be M&A, followed by greenfield investments. For Africa the expected entry modes are as presented in Table 8.4. As opposed to the entry modes in Asia and Central and Eastern Europe, geenfield investments are likely to be

Table 8.3 Expected FDI entry modes into the emerging markets, 2004–5

The figures are in percentages, indicating the percentage of the 87 international location experts surveyed in UNCTAD (2004) to give their opinions on FDI prospects, *inter alia*, for the period 2004–7.

Entry mode	**Asia**	**Central and Eastern Europe**
Mergers and acquisitions	37	40
Greenfield investments	30	42
Others*	23	18

* These will most likely be brownfield FDIs/investments.

Source: UNCTAD (2004).

Table 8.4 Expected FDI entry modes for Africa, 2004–5

The figures are in percentages, indicating the percentage of the 87 international location experts surveyed in UNCTAD (2004) to give their opinions on FDI prospects, *inter alia*, for the period 2004–7.

Entry mode	**Africa**
Mergers and acquisitions	41
Greenfield investments	42
Others*	17

* These will most likely be brownfield FDIs/investments.

Source: UNCTAD (2004).

leading entry mode to Africa. This may be explained by the presence of relatively abundant natural resources in this continent.

According to UNCTAD (2004) the Asian and Central and Eastern European emerging markets are likely to be the leading global FDI hotspots for the period 2004–7, as evidenced by Table 8.5.

FDI inflows into Africa

The African continent has been receiving the lowest share of global FDI inflows over time. According to Bjorvatn (2000:1) the whole of Africa receives less FDI than Singapore! This is despite the fact that FDI is welcomed and actively sought by virtually all African countries. The expected surge of FDI into the continent as a whole has not

Table 8.5 Global ranking of the most attractive countries for FDI inflows

Ranking	Country
Top 1	China
Top 2	India
Top 3	USA
Top 4	Thailand
Top 5	Poland
	Czech Republic
Top 6	Mexico
Top 7	Malaysia
Top 8	UK
Top 9	Singapore
	South Korea

Source: Adopted by author from UNCTAD (2004).

occurred. The continent did not benefit from the FDI boom that began in the mid-1980s.

Since 1970, FDI inflows into Africa have increased only modestly, from an annual average of almost US$1.9bn in 1983–7 to US$3.1bn in 1988–92 and US$6bn in 1993–7. For comparison purposes, note that the global FDI flows in 1998 reached a record of US$644bn (UNCTAD Press Release, 22 June 1999). The figure says much about Africa's share when we compare it with, say the US$6bn inflow to the region between 1993 and 1997. Inflows to Western Europe in 1997 were US$114,857m. and to North America the figure for the same year was US$98,994m. FDI inflows into developing countries as a group almost quadrupled from less than US$20bn in 1981–5 to US$75bn in 1991–5. Inflows to Africa in that period only two-folded. Therefore Africa's share in total inflows to developing countries dropped significantly from more than 11 per cent in 1976–80 to 9 per cent in 1981–5, 5 per cent in 1991–5 and to 4 per cent in 1996–7. Its share in total outflows from the Triad, the most important source regions for FDI flows, was even lower during the 1987–97 period as other developing regions (such as Asia, Latin America and the former communist states of Eastern and Central Europe) became more attractive as FDI locations. The share never exceeded 2 per cent until 1996. It increased to 2.4 per cent in 1997.

Africa's global FDI share is also reflected in the ratio of FDI to gross domestic product (GDP). In 1970, the region attracted more FDI per US$1000 of GDP than Asia, Latin America and the Caribbean: the FDI in dollars per US$1000 of GDP in that year was 7.9 for Africa, 6.7 for Latin America and the Caribbean, and 2.7 for South, East and South-East Asia respectively. However, the corresponding figures for 1996 were 13.6, 24.8 and 25.7, while for 1997 they were 14.7, 33.8 and 28.3 respectively. By 1990 Africa had fallen behind other developing countries in terms of its value of FDI inflows and the FDI/GDP ratio, and it has stayed behind since then. In the 1990s the gap widened when the worldwide surge in FDI flows into the developing world largely bypassed the region.

At this juncture it should be mentioned that the share of FDI flowing into Africa has not been even in all countries. Egypt and Nigeria have received the lion's share of FDIs flowing into the region in terms of absolute size. The share declined however from more than 67 per cent in 1983–7 to 54 per cent in 1988–1992 and 38 per cent in 1993–7.

Looking at the figures for FDI inflow into Africa as a whole it is clear that its global share is by all standards very low. This share needs to be increased given the potential positive roles FDI can play for the continent's development.[2] Among other things, there may be some lessons to be learned by looking at the FDI inflows into the emerging markets of Asia and Central and Eastern Europe in the context of attracting more FDIs into Africa.

Some lessons for Africa

On looking at the driving forces behind the currently impressive FDI inflows into the emerging markets of Asia and Central and Eastern Europe, it is clear that liberalization is very important. This is an important policy measure on its own. It influences almost every other FDI determinant or driving force. Besides further liberalization, the M&A entry mode has been seen to be the leading one in the emerging markets. This is not possible however without liberalization. The same applies for the other entry modes. Further liberalization is therefore required in Africa if more of the needed FDI inflows are to be realized.

Liberalization that is likely to lead to more FDI inflows should include but not necessarily be limited to the relaxation of entry restrictions in various sectors; deregulation in various industries; the abolition of price controls; privatization; the independence of the central bank; the elimination of import licensing; the removal of foreign-exchange, foreign-exchange-rate and interest-rate controls; the easing of controls over mergers and acquisitions (M&As) and trade policies.

A number of African countries are in the midst of implementing some of these far-reaching reforms in their economic management. For them to be effective in the context of attracting more FDI inflows as is the case for the emerging markets of Asia and Central and Eastern Europe, the reforms should possess the needed speed, depth and width. For example, the privatization of state monopolies should be speedier, more transparent and less bureaucratic. Liberalization programmes have to convert command-based economies into market-driven ones as has been the case in emerging markets.

Another lesson for Africa is that there is increased global competition in attracting FDIs. For example the emerging markets of Asia and Central and Eastern Europe, among other regions, are likely to be more active in promoting FDIs. As the tables above show, they are going to use further liberalization measures, additional incentives and more targeting. African countries and their development partners therefore have to be more active in promoting FDIs so as to retain the existing investors and attract new ones.

Conclusion

We may conclude here that the emerging markets of Asia and Central and Eastern Europe are becoming the new FDI hotspots. This is mainly due to drastic liberalization measures being taken by countries in these markets. Among the lessons that the African continent can learn from this is that liberalization is very important if more FDI inflows are to be attracted.

Policy recommendations

In view of the above it is recommended to policy- and decision-makers in matters pertaining to FDI that the liberalization process being implemented in a number of countries should continue. It should be a continuous, innovative and dynamic process. Besides liberalization, appropriate and necessary incentives have to be given to both actual and potential investors accordingly.

Recommendations for further research

The author has been constrained by resources from giving fuller treatment to the study topic. Further research to be recommended in this area would include the need to make firm-specific case studies to determine the driving forces behind the impressive FDI inflows into the emerging markets of Asia and Central and Eastern Europe. It would also be useful to study the specific types of liberalization measures and investment incentives that are responsible for FDI inflows into the emerging markets in our study and see whether and how these might apply in the African context.

Notes

1. These other modes of entering foreign markets include export and such arm's-length agreements like licensing, franchising and strategic partnerships.
2. The author is aware that FDI can also have some negative impacts on a host economy. In this work it is assumed that the positive impacts more than compensate the negative ones, and that therefore FDI is desirable for Africa.

References

Baumol, W.J. (1967) *Business Behaviour, Value and Growth*. New York: Macmillan.

Bjorvatn, K. (2000) 'FDI in LDC: Facts, Theory and Empirical Evidence', manuscript, Norwegian School of Economics and Business Administration (NHH) and Norwegian Centre for Research in Organisation and Management.

Caves, R.E. (1982) *Multinational Enterprises and Economic Analysis*. Cambridge University Press.

Dunning, J.H. (1992) *Multinational Enterprises and the Global Economy*. New York, NY: Addison-Wesley.

Meyer, K. and Saul, E. (1998) *Entry Mode Choice in Emerging Markets: Greenfield Acquisition and Brownfield*. Centre for East European Studies, Copenhagen Business School, Working Paper No. 18, February.

Rutherford, R.D. (1995) *Dictionary of Economics*. London: Routledge.

UNCTAD (1998) *World Investment Report*. Geneva: United Nations.

UNCTAD (2000) *World Investment Report*. Geneva: United Nations.

UNCTAD (2004) *Prospects for FDI flows, TNC Strategies and Promotion Policies: 2004–2007*. Geneva: United Nations.

9

Economic Growth and Foreign Direct Investment in the MENA Region: A Comparative Analysis

Latif Wahid

Introduction

Since the 1970s many developing countries have experienced a considerable leap towards openness and integration with neighbouring countries as well as the wider world economy. Although the significance of trade and economic blocs has become prominent in the world economy, many of the moves towards integration have not necessarily been in the form of trading blocks. Openness has been manifested in the overall change of the trading strategies of developing countries. As Cuadros *et al.* (2004) point out, the shift from an inward-looking (or import-substitution) policy to an outward-looking (or export-oriented) one has made a significant difference in the integration of the economies of the developing countries with the wider world economy. Liberalization policies in many developing countries have been part and parcel of this general process of openness. Collins *et al.* (1996) argue that during the early stages of policy change in many South-East Asian countries, including Japan, many countries maintained significant protection of their domestic market. Therefore, trade liberalization is thought to be a necessary condition for the success of an outward trade strategy, but it doesn't usually precede it.

The relationship between openness and economic growth has been investigated extensively. Recent studies (see for example Kohpaiboon 2003; Cuadros *et al.* 2004; Winters 2004) indicate that despite the econometric difficulty of establishing beyond doubt that openness enhances growth, the weight of evidence is clearly in that direction.

The openness of economies of the developing countries is expected to increase not only trade but also the flow of capital. Foreign direct investment in the past few decades has become a prominent aspect of the world economy. Many studies have indicated that in the past half-century, the volume of capital flow has been far greater than the volume of international trade. Therefore, it will be misleading to take exports and their growth as the only indicator of openness. This argument is more relevant to the case of Middle Eastern and North African (MENA) countries. Since many of these countries rely heavily on a single commodity – namely crude oil – for their export earning as well as their national well-being, their export GDP ratio seems to be high enough to merit calling them fully open economies. However, in the past three decades, MENA countries have largely failed to diversify away from oil and attract foreign investment to other spheres of their economy. Therefore, their economies have remained largely stagnant. The conclusion is that in comparison with Latin American and South-East Asian countries, MENA economies have been relatively less open and have failed to utilize their potential human and natural resources.

The aim of this chapter is not to establish the nature of the correlation between the two economic variables in MENA countries but rather to focus on their economic performance in the past two decades and subsequently on their comparative position regarding foreign capital flows. Theoretical and empirical studies on such correlation have grown considerably alongside the surge of capital inflows into the developing countries. The theme of this chapter, however, is non-technical but draws some conclusions from other technical studies.

Economic growth of the region

The MENA region includes a group of diverse and non-integrated countries, ranging from the Arab oil-exporting countries such as Saudi Arabia, Kuwait, UAE, Qatar, Iraq, Libya and Algeria, and the non-oil-based countries such as Jordan, Syria, Lebanon, Egypt, Tunisia and Morocco. It also includes the non-Arab countries of Iran,

Turkey and Israel. It is imperative, however, to mention at this stage that although MENA countries are treated largely as a group of countries, they should not be taken as sharing the same characteristics. In the past three decades, two subgroups have started to emerge within the MENA region, namely oil-based and non-oil-based countries. The distinction between the two subgroups will be examined further in the latter part of this chapter.

In comparison with the South-East Asian economies, the economic progress of the MENA region has largely been disappointing in the past three decades, except for Turkey and Israel where modest economic growth has been experienced. Expectation about economic development of the region, has however, been changing frequently in the past few decades. During the 1950s and 1960s when modern states were emerging in the Middle East, economic development through state 'socialism' was inspired by the Soviet Union, which led to the dominance of the state sector and the exclusion of the private sector from many vital sectors of the economy. This process culminated in the nationalization of oil companies in the early 1970s. Development during that period was hampered by poor human capital, agrarian problems, lack of saving and investment, and political and social tensions in the region. The rise of Arab nationalism to power during that period achieved little or no visible economic change in the region. It was during 1970s, when the price of oil quadrupled, that optimism about economic change started to revive. The understanding then prevailing was that the massive oil revenue earned by many MENA countries would help industrialization and stimulate economic growth and modernization of the region. During that decade, the region witnessed an unprecedented expansion of the construction and service sector. As Field (2000) argues, investment in infrastructure and construction was so high that at one point in the late 1970s there was as much construction underway in Saudi Arabia as in the entire USA. Unfortunately, the optimism was short-lived and economic indicators show that the average of economic growth rate has tumbled from an average of 5.42 per cent during the last half of the 1970s to a mere 1.24 per cent during the 1980s, which was lower than the average economic growth rate of the sub-Saharan African countries during the same period. The decade of the 1980s was marked by the Iran–Iraq war (1980–8), the crash of the price of oil in 1986 and the diminishing power of OPEC in the international oil market.

However, the conditions for optimism revived again in the late 1980s and early 1990s; the end of the Iran–Iraq war in 1988 and the Arab–Israeli peace plan in early 1990s were thought to mark a new era in the Middle East.

Unfortunately, close observation of the underlying factors that determine economic growth and development shows that much of the optimism arose from misdiagnosing the factors essential for economic development. The region continued to be dominated by authoritarian and non-democratic governments, while over-dependence on a single commodity – namely oil – as the main source of foreign exchange remained unchanged; military and political instability have continued and to a certain extent have worsened over time and corruption and mismanagement of resources by governments have hardly lessened. A combination of the above factors has contributed to the stagnation of the general economic condition of the whole region. Parallel to the presence of the above obstacles, external factors have not been conducive to economic and political change. Thus, While high economic and political risks have resulted in foreign investors lacking interest in investing in the region, and the instability of the international oil market has led to an erratic change in export earnings of the region, a lack of will on the part of the international community for political change in the region has exacerbated the above conditions.

It is striking to see how the economic development of the MENA region, with few exceptions, has been stagnant over the past three decades, while many South-East Asian and Latin American countries have managed to industrialize and develop. Table 9.1 shows that GDP growth of the MENA region hardly changed from the 1980s to the year 2002. The conclusion from the table is that with the exception of Turkey, a clearly declining trend can easily be observed in the economic growth of non-oil-exporting countries.

The export growth statistics show that the exports/GDP ratio declined from 37 per cent in 1970 to 34.42 per cent in the year 2002, at the time when the same ratio for East Asian and Pacific countries has more than quadrupled and that for Latin America and Caribbean countries has more than doubled. The initially relatively high exports/GDP ratio of MENA countries is attributable mainly to the heavy dependence of the region on oil exports. The export growth rates of non-oil-dependent countries such as Egypt and Israel have

Table 9.1 Basic Indicators of GDP, GDP growth rate and exports as a percentage of GDP, by region and country

Region and country	GDP[a] 2002	Percentage annual GDP growth[b] 1970	1980	1990	2002	Exports as a percentage of GDP 1970	1980	1990	2002
East Asia and Pacific	1,833,073	12.4	7.05	12.43	6.71	9.02	17.98	25.08	41.33
Latin America and Caribbean	1,668,799	6.21	6.51	−0.64	−0.79	8.95	11.54	14.08	21.29
Middle East and North Africa[b]	670,721	–	2.13	7.29	2.96	37.10	39.31	30.87	34.42
Algeria	55,914	8.86	0.79	0.80	4.10	22.07	34.34	23.44	35.79
Egypt	89,854	5.60	10.01	5.70	3.00	14.18	33.37	20.05	16.15
Israel	103,689	7.31	6.87	6.84	−0.79	27.03	43.78	34.69	30.58
Morocco	36,093	4.71	3.64	4.03	3.19	17.63	17.39	26.45	32.31
Saudi Arabia	188,479	12.03	6.52	8.33	1.02	54.48	63.55	40.63	40.78
Syria	20,783	−3.81	11.98	7.60	2.72	17.88	18.63	28.34	36.74
Tunisia	21,024	4.67	7.42	7.95	1.68	22.00	40.24	43.58	44.83
Turkey	183,665	3.23	−2.45	9.26	7.78	4.25	5.16	13.81	29.73

[a] Current US$bn.
[b] Does not include high-income economies. The economies included are: Algeria, Djibouti, Egypt, Iran, Iraq, Jordan, Lebanon, Morocco, Oman, Saudi Arabia, Syria, Tunisia, West Bank and Gaza, and Yemen.

Source: World Bank (2004a).

remained modest, while for Morocco, Tunisia and Turkey export growth has increased remarkably during the past three decades.

The general picture shows that though the debt-riddled Latin American and Caribbean countries economies have declined considerably compared with their high economic growth rate in 1970, the MENA countries' economic performance has been stagnant throughout the past quarter of a century.

Obstacles and hindrances of economic progress

Economists have long discussed the reasons behind the economic underperformance of the MENA region. Wilson (1995) attributes the failure of indigenous capitalism to develop to the strength of the traditional feudal structure, while Field (2000) argues that the failure is due largely to the nature of governance: nationalist and authoritarian governments have mismanaged resources in the past quarter of a century and have excluded foreign direct and indirect investment from the region. Others attribute the causes of economic failure to excessive military expenditure, political instability and Arab bureaucracy.

The above two approaches attribute the cause of the slow adjustment and the underperformance of the MENA economies to institutional factors. Massoud Karshenas (1999) identifies a completely different set of factors that have lead to the failure of economic development in the region. He argues that the slow pace of economic reform may have been owing to the underlying structure of these economies, arising from their resource endowment rather than to the idiosyncrasies of their political systems. He suggests that in the early 1980s, when most MENA economies were required to embark on adjustment policies to face large external negative shocks, the nature of their resource endowments limited their competitiveness and efforts to diversify away from primary commodities. At the time, the MENA countries had to compete with Latin American countries that had comparable wage levels but much greater human capital, and with highly populated South-East Asian countries which had much lower wages and much higher skills. Karshenas argues that in theory it is expected that upon trade liberalization in closed economies, wage levels will find their equilibrium value in accordance with comparative advantages of the country in question. In the MENA economies, family structures and social institution impediments have made further the downward adjustment of wages extremely difficult. In above analysis, though the reasons for the underperformance of the MENA economies are seen as lying in the nature of their factor endowments, the ability to adjust is thought to have been restricted by structural factors rather than political failure.

The social and welfare implication of the general failure of economic development is manifested in the dominance and persistence of the old political regimes and traditional value systems. While most of the countries of South-East Asia and Latin America have embraced changes and managed to industrialize to a certain extent, and to open up to foreign influence, the MENA societies have remained stagnant. Most of the economies of the region suffer from the heavy presence of the government in every sphere of the economy.

The government controls trade, allocates resources between sectors, influences income distribution through government apparatus and corrupt business practices, and distorts the general business environment through price and non-price controls.

The general masses have been excluded from the prosperity and the technological progress witnessed over the past quarter-century. Table 9.2 summarizes some general indicators in this regard. It shows that the 1980s were a difficult time for the people of the MENA region. During that decade, per capita income in the region contracted by 1.76 per cent, a greater contraction than in the countries of Africa. Compared with the South-East Asian region, which experienced a per capita income growth of 6.24 per cent during 1990s, the MENA region's growth has been disappointingly low at a time when the population growth rate during the same period has remained very high. The decline in population growth in the MENA region from the 1970s to the 1990s was negligible (9 per cent), while in South-East Asia and Latin America it was far greater (37 per cent and 32 per cent, respectively). The obvious implication of this trend is lower standards of living, high rates of unemployment and a continuous brain drain from the region.

Table 9.2 Per capita income and population growth by region, 1970s–2000

				Percentage growth rates					
	Population	*Per capita income*[b]		Population			Per capita income		
Region	2000[a]	1980	2000	1970s	1980s	1990s	1970s	1980s	1990s
East Asia and Pacific	1,805	297	949	2.09	1.61	1.31	5.0	5.69	6.24
Latin America and Caribbean	510	3519	3808	2.45	2.03	1.66	3.3	−0.16	1.20
Middle East and North Africa	294	2072	2050	2.59	3.13	2.35	–	−1.76	1.36
Sub-Saharan African countries	638	660	566	2.80	2.92	2.64	–	−0.67	−0.65

[a] Millions.
[b] GDP per capita income (constant 1995 US$).
Source: World Bank (2004a).

Foreign direct investments and economic growth

The potential relationship between economic growth and foreign resource flows has been debated and investigated widely. Many economists believe that resource inflow in the form of foreign direct investment (FDI) augments local resources and may help to raise economic growth. Other benefits of FDI are thought to be technological diffusion and the transfer of managerial know-how to developing countries. However, many argue that the benefits can be realized only when recipient countries provide suitable conditions for FDI. Hermes and Lensink (2003) investigated the role of the development of the financial system in enhancing the positive relationship between FDI and economic growth in 67 developing countries, including most of the African and Latin American countries and 15 Asian countries. They found that of the 67 countries, 37 had a sufficiently developed financial system to let FDI contribute positively to economic growth. Almost every other country was in sub-Saharan Africa where weak financial systems had not stimulated a positive relationship between FDI and economic growth. The experience of China in the past two decades has shown that the development of the financial system is not the only condition for the presence of such a relationship. While the Chinese financial system is far less developed than that of its neighbours and some Latin American countries, most foreign investment flow into China during the 1990s was as FDI. The other contrasting example is Brazil, which is regarded as having been the largest recipient of portfolio capital during 1990s but still maintained a very restrictive policy towards FDI. This also shows that country-specific conditions may attract one type of capital inflow but not necessarily all types simultaneously. Bosworth *et al.* (1999) argue that, increasingly, the three types of capital inflows (FDI, portfolio investment and loans) are not significantly correlated with one another over time.

The other important precondition for high capital inflow, particularly among the South-East Asian countries, has been government polices that stimulate saving and investment and favour trade liberalization alongside extensive intervention in some sectors of the economy. However, in South-East Asia government policies towards FDI inflows have not been the same. Collins *et al.* (1996) argue that every country has shifted away from an inward-looking development strategy toward an outward-oriented one, and has encouraged capital goods imports, licensing arrangements and training abroad, foreign direct investment was welcomed in some countries such as Malaysia, Singapore, and more recently in Indonesia and Thailand, but was heavily restricted in Taiwan especially South Korea.

Table 9.3 shows that economic growth in the MENA countries during the 1980s and 1990s was 1.43 per cent and 3.75 per cent respectively. The average growth rate in the MENA and Latin American economies was less than a third that in the South-East Asian economies during the same period. However, within the MENA economies, the non-oil-based economies have experienced less-erratic changes in economic growth rates. For instance in Egypt, Israel, Jordan, Morocco, Tunisia and Turkey economic growth was above 3.5 per cent during the same two decades. The erratic growth rates in the oil economies can be traced to the volatile international oil market. In the last three years of the survey the growth rates of all three groups of countries slowed down. However, in the Latin American and MENA economies the slowdown was considerably greater than in those of South-East Asia.

Foreign direct investment inflows during the past two decades may shed some light on the slow economic growth of the MENA economies. Table 9.4 shows that during 1980s the countries of Latin America attracted more FDI than did those of South-East Asia and the MENA. The surge of FDI during 1990s into South-East Asia and Latin America was phenomenal at a time when FDI into the MENA economies declined from an annual average of US$3,978bn during the 1980s to US$2,998 bn. Within the group, the non-oil-based economies seem to have attracted more foreign capital than the others. The figures for the 1990s show that Egypt, Morocco and Tunisia together attracted an average 55.4 per cent of total FDI into region. Their share increased during the last three years of the survey to 98 per cent, 65 per cent and 70 per cent respectively. The other striking evidence from the figures is the amount of FDI into Israel and Turkey. The two countries attracted about 63.5 per cent of the total annual FDI inflows into the whole region.

However, over the two decades, the share of the MENA region in total FDI inflows into all developing countries declined noticeably. While the region attracted about 37 per cent of the total FDI into all developing countries during the first half of 1980s, the average share had, according to the *World Bank Investment Report* (2004), declined to about 2 per cent during 1995–2002.

Table 9.3 Economic growth rates by region and country, 1980–2002

Region and country	Growth rates				
	1980s	1990s	2000	2001	2002
South-East Asia and Pacific	7.39	7.63	7.10	5.65	6.71
Latin America and Caribbean	2.02	2.89	3.67	0.28	−0.79
MENA	1.43	3.75	4.28	3.33	2.96
Algeria	2.80	1.57	2.40	2.60	4.10
Egypt	5.86	4.40	5.11	3.50	3.00
Iran	0.01	4.72	5.93	4.81	6.71
Israel	3.66	5.39	7.53	−0.91	−0.79
Jordan	3.98	4.88	4.28	4.25	4.86
Morocco	4.47	2.73	0.96	6.30	3.20
Saudi Arabia	−0.62	3.10	4.86	1.31	1.02
Syria	2.84	5.92	0.60	7.19	2.72
Tunisia	3.56	5.05	4.67	4.86	1.68
Turkey	4.08	3.89	7.36	−7.49	7.78
UAE	1.23	4.58	12.30	3.50	1.80

Source: World Bank (2004a).

Table 9.4 FDI inflows, by region and country, 1980–2002 (US$m.)

Host region and Country	Annual average				
	1980s	1990s	2000	2001	2002
East Asia and Pacific	3,667	45,465	44,204	48,204	54,833
Latin America and Caribbean	6,128	38,180	76,961	69,948	44,682
MENA[a]	3,978	2,998	2,438	5,796	2,653
Algeria	34	187	438	1,196	1,065
Egypt	859	746	1,235	510	647
Iran	−48	3	39	50	37
Israel	126	1,132	4,988	3,520	1,649
Jordan	46	91	787	100	56
Lebanon	1	77	297	249	257
Morocco	61	558	423	2,808	428
Syria	30	113	270	205	225
Tunisia	157	356	752	457	795
Turkey	168	772	982	3,266	1,037

[a] Does not include high middle-income countries.

Source: World Bank (2004b).

The regional distribution of FDI discussed above shows that international investment has been attracted to the region when economic growth has been reasonably high and when export orientation policies have been adopted. The last factor has usually been accompanied by a stable political and economic environment. De Mello (1997) argues that the most important factors in the surge of FDI inflows into the developing countries have been the foreign acquisition of domestic firms in the process of privatization, the globalization of production, and increased economic and financial integration. The MENA region economies have so far failed to create the appropriate economic and political environment to attract foreign direct and indirect investments. The political environment at the beginning of twenty-first century is no better than the conditions prevailing during the rise of Arab nationalism to power during the 1960s and 1970s. Parallel to this, the general openness of the region to international trade and competition has not been materialized into the rise of competitive non-oil exports. Wilson (1995) argues that, although increasing economic openness is a feature of most economies in the region, this is consumption-led rather than production-led. As discussed already, the MENA economies have in most cases remained heavily dependent on exports of crude oil; FDI is attracted to this capital-intensive sector. It is also noted that with the exception of the Gulf oil states, most of the MENA countries have maintained foreign exchange control. As Safadi (1997) points out, in most MENA countries FDI is governed by a variety of laws and regulations. The conditions have been worsened by the weakness of the banking and financial system, the lack of transparency, corruption, and out-of-date business practices.

The failure to attract foreign capital has been coupled with the failure of regional economic integration and inward investment. Wilson (1998) points out that progress regarding economic integration between Arab countries has been limited. The Arab common market could not be effective because its members have little to offer each other in terms of traded goods and most of the countries of the region, apart from the Gulf oil states, maintain foreign exchange control. Political and military conflicts between countries have also limited the scope for economic integration and economic cooperation. The area's most advanced economy, Israel, is boycotted by many of its neighbours, and consequently has developed bilateral trade deals with Europe and the USA rather within the region.

The general conclusion is that the dominance and the presence of the state sector in every sphere of the economy, except in Turkey and Israel, has rendered private sectors weak and uncompetitive, and the general economic and political conditions for FDI unsuitable. In most of the oil-based economies, FDI has occurred through the government sector and into the capital-intensive oil industry. The surge of investment into Algeria in the past few years is a testimony to this observation. Many countries with a potential for FDI, such as Iran and Iraq, have attracted little or none, largely because of their political and military instability.

Concluding remarks

In the light of the political and institutional obstacles to economic growth discussed in this chapter, the MENA region is faced with a daunting challenge. In comparison with the South-East Asian and Latin American countries, growth in the MENA economies was very poor in the past three decades. The main impediments to economic progress seem to have been structural and institutional weakness, the dominance of the state sector, heavy dependence on the export of a single primary commodity – namely oil – and political and social instability.

There is no doubt that the region's ability to draw upon an international pool of capital offers large potential economic benefits. However, the overall conditions have rendered the region unattractive to FDI. To rise to the challenge of modernization, the MENA countries have to address the aforementioned impediments to economic progress. In the long term, a shift is required in government policies, away from political and ideological rhetoric and towards providing the necessary conditions for economic development.

References

Bosworth, B.P. and S.M. Collins (1999) *Capital Flows to Developing Economies: Implications for Saving and Investment*, Brookings Papers on Economic Activity, 1 (1999). Washington, DC: Brookings Institution, 143–69.

Collins, S.M., B.P. Bosworth and D. Rodrik (1996) '*Economic Growth in East Asia: Accumulation versus Assimilation*, Brookings Papers on Economic Activity, 2 (1996). Washington, DC: Brookings Institution, 135–91.

Cuadros, A., V. Orts and M. Alguacil (2004) 'Openness and Growth: Re-Examining Foreign Direct Investment, Trade and Output Linkages in Latin America', *Journal of Development Studies*, 40(4), 167–92.

De Mello, L.R. (1997) 'Foreign Direct Investment in Developing Countries and Growth: A Selected Survey', *Journal of Development studies*, 34(1), 1–34.

Field, M. (2000) 'What Are the Prospects for Modernizing the Middle East Economies?', in Wright, J.W. and L. Drake (ed.), *Economic and Political Impediments to Middle East Peace*. New Zealand: Macmillan.

Hermes, N. and R. Lensink (2003) 'Foreign Direct Investment, Financial Development and Economic Growth', *Journal of Development Studies*, 40(1), 142–63.

Karshenas, M. (1999) *Structural Obstacles to Economic Adjustment in the MENA Region: The International Trade Aspects*, School of Oriental and African Studies, University of London, Working Paper no. 88.

Kohpaiboon, A. (2003) 'Foreign Trade Regimes and the FDI-Growth Nexus: A Case Study of Thailand', *Journal of Development Studies*, 40(2), 55–69.

Safadi, R. (1997) 'Global Challenges and Opportunities Facing MENA Countries at the Dawn of the Twenty-First Century', in Handoussa, H. (ed.), *Economic Transition in the Middle East*. American University in Cairo Press, pp. 19–41.

Wilson, R. (1995) *Economic Development in the Middle East*. London: Routledge.

Wilson, R. (1998) 'The Contribution by Economists to Middle Eastern Studies (1973–1998)', *British Journal of Middle Eastern Studies*, 25(2), 235–46.

Winters, L.A. 2004 'Trade Liberalization and Economic Performance: An Overview', *Economic Journal*, 114(493), F4.

World Bank (2004a) *World Development Indicators*. April. Washington, DC.

World Bank (2004b) *World investment Indicators*. April. Washington, DC.

Index

Africa, ix, 145, 157, 159
Akaike's Information Criteria (AIC), 19
Albania, 66, 69, 80
Algeria, ix, 3, 115, 117–20, 122, 124, 164, 167
Argentina, 14, 16–18
Armenia, 66, 68, 79, 80, 85, 93
Augmented Dickey–Fuller (ADF), 10, 11, 20
autoregressive distributed lags, vii, 12, 21, 23, 25
Azerbaijan, 66, 68, 79, 80, 85

band
  period, 30
  regime, 30
bandwagon, 56
banks, 14, 15, 27–30, 32–4, 38, 40
  central bank, 142, 160
  crisis, 29, 31, 41, 50, 55, 58, 95, 98–103, 105, 106, 112, 116
bargaining
  blind, 63, 76, 77, 82, 86, 87
  irrelevance, 75
  models, 76
  obsolescing, 76
  outcome, 63
  power, 75
  relations, 76
Belarus, 66–8, 70, 74, 78, 79, 80, 85, 86, 91
Bosnia and Herzegovina, 69, 80
Brazil, 14, 16, 17
Bulgaria, 66, 67, 69, 80, 84, 85

capital
  flows, vii, viii, xvii, xviii, 1, 2, 7, 15, 22, 26, 29–57, 61, 62, 74, 89, 164
  inflows, vii, xi, 2, 9, 14, 16–26, 35, 40–43, 48, 51, 56, 62, 64, 164, 170
  outflows, 32
Caribbean, 159, 166, 167, 169, 172
Chile, 14, 16–18
cointegration, 7, 12, 18–20, 26, 27, 144
Colombia, 14, 16
conglomerates, 152
corporate governance, 6, 156
correlation coefficient, 17, 36, 38, 40, 49, 51
corruption, 14, 26, 71, 73, 78, 79, 90, 140, 166, 173
country risk, 3, 62, 64, 82, 89, 90
crawling peg, 30
Croatia, 66, 69, 80
cross-border merger and acquisitions, 152
cumulative capital outflows, 32, 35, 51, 56
currency, ix, 15, 96, 100, 101, 108–11
  appreciation, 42, 49, 56
  arrangement, 30
  band, 29, 35, 51
  bond, 51
  controls, 100
  convertibility, 77
  denomination, 51
  depreciation, 41
  exposure, ix, 96, 101, 107–11
  fluctuation, 3
  foreign, 15, 51, 101
  management, 106
  regime, 30, 49
  risk, 95, 96, 98, 108, 109, 111, 112
  run, 58

currency – *continued*
transaction, viii, 102, 104, 106, 112
translation, 104–6, 112
cyclical
anti-, 58
pro-, 58
Cyprus, 124
Czech Republic, 65, 66, 67, 69, 80, 84, 85, 149, 158

debt, 64, 167
crisis, 29, 56, 116
non-private, 15
per capita, 82, 86, 88
private, 15
sovereign, ii
terms of, 115
disinflation, 42
driving forces, 4, 51, 145, 149, 151, 153, 156–9, 161
dynamic models, ii, 2, 9, 12, 26, 28, 117, 154, 160

Egypt, 124, 144, 159, 164, 166–7, 171–2
emerging
economies, vii, xvii, xviii, 1, 2, 9, 10, 14, 18, 19
markets (EMs), ii, iv, ix, xi, xvii, 1, 4, 7, 17, 18, 26, 127, 145, 148, 151, 156–61
endogenous, 89
Estonia, 66, 68, 80, 84, 85
Euro, 117
exchange rate
band, 40
fixed, 30, 39, 49, 56
flexible, 2
floating, 29
foreign, ix, 109–11, 160
regime, ii, xvii, 2, 29, 30, 41
risks, 150
exposure
currency, ix, 96, 101, 106, 108–11
economic, 95, 96, 103
foreign exchange, 103
managed, viii, ix, 109
transaction, viii, 102, 104–6, 112
translation, 104–6, 112

financial
development, vii, xvii, xviii, 1, 2, 5–9, 14–26
institutions, ii, 5
instruments, 95, 96, 106, 155
liberalization, 6–8
losses, 95, 99, 103
markets, 5, 22, 62, 103, 154
statistics, 128–32
system, 6, 8, 170, 173
fluctuation
in capital flows, xvii, 30
currency, 3
short-term, 2, 31, 57
wild, 95
foreign direct investment, v, vi, viii, xvii, 15, 22, 61, 66, 90, 92, 115, 123, 128, 131–3, 139, 144, 146, 163, 164, 170, 171, 175
benign FDI, 62, 64, 75, 82, 86, 87
malign FDI, 62, 63, 75, 77, 82

Georgia, 66, 68, 78–80, 85, 91
global
competition, 75, 77, 160
distribution, 145
FDI, 67, 70, 148, 157, 159
GDP, 67
inflows, 70
markets, 147
risk, xv
trend, 120, 149
globalization, 61, 173
globalizing economy, 154
growth, vi, ix, x, 1, 4, 8, 27, 28, 41, 42, 52, 54, 59, 62, 63, 65, 73, 74, 76, 88, 89, 92, 115, 116, 123–33, 142, 145, 147, 148, 152, 156, 161, 163–75

heterogeneity, 9–12, 26–8
horizontal
FDI, 136, 143
M&As, 152
Hungary, 66–9, 80, 84, 85

imperfect competition, 135, 136
inefficiency, 72
inflation, 31, 32, 39, 42, 49, 58, 64, 82, 88
  disinflation, 42, 44
infrastructure, 61, 71, 89, 118, 134, 147, 165
instability, 3, 32, 36, 58, 62, 63, 70, 73, 75, 77, 87, 102, 166, 168, 174
integration, vii, 9, 26, 147, 163, 173
  disintegration, 77
interest rate
  controls, 160
  futures, 103
  nominal, 31, 37, 41, 42, 46–8, 54, 55, 58
  real, 31, 42, 45, 48, 49, 53, 54, 58
  risk, 99, 101, 103
  subsidies, 150
International Country Risk Guide (ICRG), 14, 93
international trade, 134–7, 143, 164, 173
Iran, 164–7, 172, 174
Iraq, 164–7, 174
Israel, 165–7, 171, 172–4

Jamaica, 14, 16, 18
Japan, 72, 138, 144, 145, 163
Jordan, 14, 16, 18

Kazakhstan, 66, 68, 70, 73, 78, 79, 80, 85, 91
Korea, 14, 16–18, 149, 159, 171
Kuwait, 164
Kyiv, 72, 92
Kyrgyzstan, 66, 68, 70, 74, 79, 80, 85, 91

lags, 12, 19, 31, 37, 38, 44, 45, 52, 54, 55, 58
Latin America, xvii, 58, 59, 148, 149, 158, 159, 164, 166–8, 170, 171, 172, 174, 175
Latvia, 66, 68, 70, 84, 85
least square dummy variable (LSDV), 83, 84
Lebanon, 124, 168, 172
Libya, 144, 164
likelihood
  log, 19, 21, 23–25
  maximum, 13
liquid liability, xi, 14–17, 19, 21, 23–5
Lithuania, 66, 68, 70, 84, 85
LM bar test, 9, 10
loans, 15, 29, 30, 32–4, 36, 115, 116, 150, 170

Macedonia, 66, 69, 80
macroeconomics, v, 29–59, 138
Malaysia, v, xiii, 3, 14, 16–18, 95–108, 119, 149, 158, 171
Malta, 124
merger and acquisitions (M&As), 154
  horizontal, 152
  vertical, 152
Mexico, v, vii, viii, xiii, xvii, 2, 14, 16 18, 29–59, 90, 91, 149, 159
Middle East and North African (MENA), vi, 4, 119, 163
Moldova, 64, 66–8, 73, 78–80, 85, 86, 91
Morocco, ix, 3, 115, 117, 118, 120–30, 132, 144, 164, 167, 171, 172
multinational corporations (MNCs), 75, 116, 147
multinational enterprises (MNEs), xii, 3, 75, 89, 147

Nigeria, 159

offshore, 142
OLS (ordinary least squares), 82–4, 140
Oman, 167

panel unit root, vii, 9, 18, 19
Peru, 14, 16, 17
Philippines, 14, 16–18
Poland, 66, 67, 69, 80, 84, 85, 149, 159
pooled mean group (PMG) estimator, 12–16, 19–25
portfolio, 8, 15, 16, 22, 29, 30, 35, 56, 170

Qatar, 164
quota, 150

restrictions, 153, 170
regulation, 74, 79, 115, 118, 127, 155
risk, ii, viii, ix, 1, 3, 14, 62, 71, 82, 87, 92, 95–115
Romania, 66, 68, 80, 84, 85
Russia, 65–7, 70–2, 79, 80, 85, 86, 91

Saudi Arabia, 164, 167
Serbia and Montenegro, 69, 80
Slovakia, 66, 68, 80, 84, 85
sovereignty, ii, 89
specification, 8, 13, 22, 43, 45, 52–6, 138
standardized coefficient/distribution, 11, 82, 84, 98
stationarity, 13, 18, 19, 126
statistics, vii, 9–11, 14, 16, 18–25, 33, 70, 124, 166
structure, 62, 70, 82, 90
Syria, 124, 164, 167, 172

Tajikistan, 66, 70, 80, 85, 86
target, 3, 62, 65, 72, 82, 85, 118, 124, 149–51, 155, 160
tariffs, 136, 146, 150
technological leadership, 154
Thailand, 14, 16–18, 149, 159, 171, 175
trade, v, vi, xi, xvii, 1, 4, 7, 65, 72, 133–50, 164, 175
- agreement, 35, 134
- balance, 64, 82, 83, 85–7
- credit, 15
- flows, 143
- free, 123
- international, 27, 134, 135, 144, 164, 173, 175
- liberalization, 7, 59, 127, 159, 163, 164, 170
- openness, xvi, xvii, 2, 8, 9, 14, 16–19, 21–6
- strategy, 163
- volume, 64
- world, 117

transparency, 77–80, 82, 89, 91, 173
Tunisia, v, xi, 3, 4, 115, 117, 120, 122–4, 126, 130–50, 167, 170–2
Turkey, 14, 16, 17, 124, 165–7, 171, 172, 174
Turkmenistan, 66, 70, 85, 86

UAE, 164, 172
Ukraine, 64–8, 72, 73, 77–80, 86, 90–3
uncertainty, 3, 63, 76, 78, 87, 103
UNCTAD, 65, 66, 69, 70, 91, 117–22, 132–4, 143, 144, 146–53, 155–9
unpredictability, 77, 100
unrestricted
- autoregression, 12
- errors, 12
- model, 20
- OLS, 82, 83

Uruguay, 14, 16, 17
Uzbekistan, 66, 70, 78, 79, 80, 85, 86, 93

VAR (vector autoregressive), 40
variance, 7, 10, 11, 20
Venezuela, 14, 16, 17
volatility, 29, 35, 36, 56, 59, 105

West Bank, 167
World Bank, 14, 27, 28, 73, 119, 120, 128–30, 132, 167, 169
World Development Indicators, 15

Yemen, 167